Cybertext

Perspectives on Ergodic Literature

Espen J. Aarseth

THE JOHNS HOPKINS UNIVERSITY PRESS ■ BALTIMORE AND LONDON

© 1997 The Johns Hopkins University Press
All rights reserved. Published 1997
Printed in the United States of America on acid-free paper

06 05 04 03 02 01 00 99 98 97   5 4 3 2 1

The Johns Hopkins University Press
2715 North Charles Street
Baltimore, Maryland 21218–4319
The Johns Hopkins Press Ltd., London

Library of Congress Cataloging-in-Publication Data will be found
at the end of this book.
A catalog record for this book is available from the British Library.

ISBN 0–8018–5578–0
ISBN 0–8018–5579–9 (pbk.)

Title page illustration: The design is the 811th generation of the stairstep hexomino, which was automatically evolved using Andrew Trevorrow's program LifeLab (with the 3–4 rule) from the initial state ▮▮▪ .

A World Wide Web site for this book can be found at
http://www.hf.uib.no/cybertext/
It contains links to many of the texts and computer programs discussed, as well as pointers to other relevant resources.

Literature is a combinatorial game that pursues the possibilities implicit in its own material, independent of the personality of the poet, but it is a game that at a certain point is invested with an unexpected meaning, a meaning that is not patent on the linguistic plane on which we were working but has slipped in from another level, activating something that on that second level is of great concern to the author or his society. The literature machine can perform all the permutations possible on a given material, but the poetic result will be the particular effect of one of these permutations on a man endowed with a consciousness and an unconscious, that is, an empirical and historical man. It will be the shock that occurs only if the writing machine is surrounded by the hidden ghosts of the individual and his society.

ITALO CALVINO

This work was made possible by a three-year Ph.D. scholarship from the Norwegian Research Council. I wish to thank the Faculty of Arts, University of Bergen, for their generosity in providing me with basic equipment crucial to my project, when they were under no obligation to do so.

A large number of people in various countries have contributed invaluable help and inspiration during my years of research. By naming none, I hope to include all. I am indebted to my supervisors, Atle Kittang and Richard Holton Pierce, for their critical and inspiring support. I am also very grateful to my colleagues and friends at the Humanities Computing Section, in particular Roald Skarsten.

C Y B E R T E X T

One Introduction: Ergodic Literature

The Book and the Labyrinth

A few words on the two neoteric terms, *cybertext* and *ergodic*, are in order. *Cybertext* is a neologism derived from Norbert Wiener's book (and discipline) called *Cybernetics*, and subtitled *Control and Communication in the Animal and the Machine* (1948). Wiener laid an important foundation for the development of digital computers, but his scope is not limited to the mechanical world of transistors and, later, of microchips. As the subtitle indicates, Wiener's perspective includes both organic and inorganic systems; that is, any system that contains an information feedback loop. Likewise, the concept of cybertext does not limit itself to the study of computer-driven (or "electronic") textuality; that would be an arbitrary and unhistorical limitation, perhaps comparable to a study of literature that would only acknowledge texts in paper-printed form. While there might be sociological reasons for such a study, we would not be able to claim any understanding of how different forms of literature vary.

The concept of cybertext focuses on the mechanical organization of the text, by positing the intricacies of the medium as an integral part of the literary exchange. However, it also centers attention on the consumer, or user, of the text, as a more integrated figure than even reader-response theorists would claim. The performance of their reader takes place all in his head, while the user of cybertext also performs in an extranoematic sense. During the cybertextual process, the user will have effectuated a semiotic sequence, and this selective movement is a work of physical construction that the various concepts of "reading" do not account for. This phenomenon I call *ergodic*, using a term appropriated from physics that derives from the Greek words *ergon* and *hodos*, meaning "work" and "path." In ergodic literature, nontrivial effort is required to allow the reader to traverse the text. If ergodic literature is to make sense as a concept, there must also be nonergodic literature, where the effort to traverse the text is trivial, with no extranoematic responsibilities placed on

1

the reader except (for example) eye movement and the periodic or arbitrary turning of pages.

Whenever I have had the opportunity to present the perspective of ergodic literature and cybertext to a fresh audience of literary critics and theorists, I have almost invariably been challenged on the same issues: that these texts (hypertexts, adventure games, etc.) aren't essentially different from other literary texts, because (1) all literature is to some extent indeterminate, nonlinear, and different for every reading, (2) the reader has to make choices in order to make sense of the text, and finally (3) a text cannot really be non-linear because the reader can read it only one sequence at a time, anyway.

Typically, these objections came from persons who, while well versed in literary theory, had no firsthand experience of the hyper-texts, adventure games, or multi-user dungeons I was talking about. At first, therefore, I thought this was simply a didactical problem: if only I could present examples of my material more clearly, every-thing would become indisputable. After all, can a person who has never seen a movie be expected to understand the unique character-istics of that medium? A text such as the *I Ching* is not meant to be read from beginning to end but entails a very different and highly specialized ritual of perusal, and the text in a multi-user dungeon is without either beginning or end, an endless labyrinthine plateau of textual bliss for the community that builds it. But no matter how hard I try to describe these texts to you, the reader, their essential difference will remain a mystery until they are experienced first-hand.

In my campaign for the study of cybertextuality I soon real-ized that my terminology was a potential source of confusion. Par-ticularly problematic was the word *nonlinear.* For some it was a common literary concept used to describe narratives that lacked or subverted a straightforward story line; for others, paradoxically, the word could not describe my material, since the act of reading must take place sequentially, word for word.

This aporia never ceased to puzzle me. There was obviously an epistemological conflict. Part of the problem is easily resolved: hypertexts, adventure games, and so forth are not texts the way the average literary work is a text. In what way, then, are they texts? They produce verbal structures, for aesthetic effect. This makes them similar to other literary phenomena. But they are also something more, and it is this added paraverbal dimension that is so hard to see. A cybertext is a machine for the production of variety of expression. Since literary theorists are trained to uncover literary ambivalence in texts with linear expression, they evidently mistook texts with variable expression for texts with ambiguous meaning. When confronted with a forking text such as a hypertext, they claimed that all texts are produced as a linear sequence during reading, so where was my problem?

The problem was that, while they focused on what was being read, I focused on what was being read *from*. This distinction is inconspicuous in a linear expression text, since when you read from *War and Peace*, you believe you are reading *War and Peace*. In drama, the relationship between a play and its (varying) performance is a hierarchical and explicit one; it makes trivial sense to distinguish between the two. In a cybertext, however, the distinction is crucial—and rather different; when you read from a cybertext, you are constantly reminded of inaccessible strategies and paths not taken, voices not heard. Each decision will make some parts of the text more, and others less, accessible, and you may never know the exact results of your choices; that is, exactly what you missed. This is very different from the ambiguities of a linear text. And inaccessibility, it must be noted, does not imply ambiguity but, rather, an absence of possibility—an aporia.

So why is this so difficult to see? Why is the variable expression of the nonlinear text so easily mistaken for the semantic ambiguity of the linear text? The answer, or at least one answer, can be found in a certain rhetorical model used by literary theory. I refer to the idea of a narrative text as a labyrinth, a game, or an imaginary world, in which the reader can explore at will, get lost, discover secret paths, play around, follow the rules, and so on. The problem with these powerful metaphors, when they begin to affect the critic's perspective and judgment, is that they enable a systematic misrepresentation of the relationship between narrative text and reader; a spatiodynamic fallacy where the narrative is not perceived as a presentation of a world but rather as that world itself. In other words, there is a short circuit between signifier and signified, a suspension of *différance* that projects an objective level beyond the text, a primary metaphysical structure that generates both textual sign and our understanding of it, rather than the other way around.

A reader, however strongly engaged in the unfolding of a narrative, is powerless. Like a spectator at a soccer game, he may speculate, conjecture, extrapolate, even shout abuse, but he is not a player. Like a passenger on a train, he can study and interpret the shifting landscape, he may rest his eyes wherever he pleases, even release the emergency brake and step off, but he is not free to move the tracks in a different direction. He cannot have the player's pleasure of influence: "Let's see what happens when I do *this*." The reader's pleasure is the pleasure of the voyeur. Safe, but impotent.

The cybertext reader, on the other hand, is not safe, and therefore, it can be argued, she is not a reader. The cybertext puts its would-be reader at risk: the risk of rejection. The effort and energy demanded by the cybertext of its reader raise the stakes of interpretation to those of intervention. Trying to know a cybertext is an investment of personal improvisation that can result in either intimacy or failure. The tensions at work in a cybertext, while not incompatible with those of narrative desire, are also something more: a struggle not merely for interpretative insight but also for narrative control: "I want this text to tell *my* story; the story that *could not be* without me." In some cases this is literally true. In other cases, perhaps most, the sense of individual outcome is illusory, but nevertheless the aspect of coercion and manipulation is real.

The study of cybertexts reveals the misprision of the spacio-dynamic metaphors of narrative theory, because ergodic literature incarnates these models in a way linear text narratives do not. This may be hard to understand for the traditional literary critic who cannot perceive the difference between metaphorical structure and logical structure, but it is essential. The cybertext reader *is* a player, a gambler; the cybertext *is* a game-world or world-game; it *is* possible to explore, get lost, and discover secret paths in these texts, not metaphorically, but through the topological structures of the textual machinery. This is not a difference between games and literature but rather between games and narratives. To claim that there is no difference between games and narratives is to ignore essential qualities of both categories. And yet, as this study tries to show, the difference is not clear-cut, and there is significant overlap between the two.

It is also essential to recognize that *cybertext* is used here to describe a broad textual media category. It is not in itself a literary genre of any kind. Cybertexts share a principle of calculated production, but beyond that there is no obvious unity of aesthetics, thematics, literary history, or even material technology. Cybertext is a perspective I use to describe and explore the communicational strategies of dynamic texts. To look for traditions, literary genres, and common aesthetics, we must inspect the texts at a much more local level, and I suggest one way to partition the field in chapters 4 through 7, each chapter dealing with a subgroup of ergodic textuality.

Even if the cybertexts are not narrative texts but other forms of literature governed by a different set of rules, they retain to a lesser or greater extent some aspects of narrative. Most display some forms of narrative behavior, just as can be found in other nonnarrative literary genres. The idea of pure literary forms or discrete genres is not be pursued here. Instead, a perspective of complementary generic traits is used to describe the various types as synthetic, composite genres. Perhaps, by studying cybertexts and trying to discover this alterity of narrative, we may also get some small new clues as to what narrative is.

It seems to me that the cybertexts fit the game-world-labyrinth terminology in a way that exposes its deficiencies when used on narrative texts. But how has the spatiodynamic misrepresentation of narrative originated? And was it always inappropriate? An important clue to this question can be found in the historical idea of the labyrinth. Our present idea of the labyrinth is the Borgesian structure of "forking paths," the bewildering chaos of passages that lead in many directions but never directly to our desired goal. But there is also another kind, or paradigm, of labyrinths. Penelope Reed Doob, in her excellent discussion of physical and metaphorical labyrinths of classical antiquity and the Middle Ages (1990), distinguishes between two kinds of labyrinthine structure: the unicursal, where there is only one path, winding and turning, usually toward a center; and the multicursal, where the maze wanderer faces a series of critical choices, or bivia.

Umberto Eco (1984, 80) claims that there are three types of labyrinth: the linear, the maze, and the net (or rhizome; cf. Deleuze and Guattari 1987). The first two correspond to Doob's unicursal and multicursal, respectively. To include the net seems inappropriate, since this structure has very different qualities from the other two. Especially as the net's "every point can be connected with every other point" (Eco 1984, 81); this is exactly the opposite of the fundamental inaccessibility of the other models. Amazingly, Eco also claims that the labyrinth of Crete was linear and that Theseus "had no choices to make: he could not but reach the center, and from the center, the way out. . . . In this kind of labyrinth the Ariadne thread is useless, since one *cannot* get lost" (80). It is hard to believe that Eco is speaking of the labyrinth where Theseus, famously, was the first to find the way out, and only because of Ariadne's thread. This was the same complex labyrinth where even its maker, Daedalus, was lost. Doob (1990, 17–38), on the other hand, citing Pliny, Virgil, Ovid, and others, shows that the literary tradition describes the *Domus daedali* as a multicursal labyrinth.

As Doob demonstrates, the labyrinth as a sign of complex artistry, inextricability, and difficult process was an important metaphor and motif in classical and medieval literature, philosophy, rhetoric, and visual design. Paradoxically, while the labyrinth depicted in visual art from prehistoric times is always unicursal, the literary maze (with the Cretan myth as the chief example) is usually multicursal. The multicursal motif did not appear in art until the Renaissance, but as Doob shows, the two paradigms coexisted peacefully as the same concept at least since Virgil (70–19 B.C.). In Doob's view, what to us seem to be contradictory models were subsumed in a single category, signifying a complex design, artistic order *and* chaos (depending on point of view), inextricability or impenetrability, and the difficult progress from confusion to perception. Both models share these essential qualities of the labyrinth, and apparently there was no great need to distinguish between the two.

In the Renaissance, however, the idea of the labyrinth, both in literature and visual art, was reduced to the multicursal paradigm that we recognize today. Consequently, the old metaphor of the text as labyrinth, which in medieval poetics could signify both a difficult, winding, but potentially rewarding linear process *and* a spatial, artistically complex, and confusing artifact, was restricted to the latter sense. Therefore, I find it reasonable to assume that the image of the text as a labyrinth has undergone an ideological transformation, from a harmonic duality where the figurative likeness of the narrative text as unicursal coexisted with a tropology of multicursal aspects, such as repetition, interlaced narrative threads, prolepsis, and so forth. When the unicursal paradigm faded, however, the multicursal paradigm came to dominate the figure, devolving the rich ambiguity of the classical and medieval labyrinth into the less ambiguous Renaissance model of pure multicursality.

Since we now regard *labyrinthine* and *linear* as incompatible terms, and since the labyrinth no longer denotes linear progress and teleology but only their opposites, its status as a model of narrative text has become inapt for most narratives. For a typical example of this misnomer, consider the following, from a discussion of postmodernist writing: "We shall never be able to unravel the plots of John Fowles's *The Magus* (1966), Alain Robbe-Grillet's *Le Voyeur* (1955) or Thomas Pynchon's *The Crying of Lot 49* (1966), for they are *labyrinths without exits*" (Lodge 1977, 266; last italics mine). Here, the image of the labyrinth has become severely distorted. A labyrinth without exit is a labyrinth without entrance; in other words, not a labyrinth at all.

Even in highly subversive narratives, such as the novels of Samuel Beckett or Italo Calvino's *If on a Winter's Night a Traveler . . .* (1993), the reader is faced, topologically, with a unicursal maze. Yet there are some novels for which the post-Renaissance model is perfectly valid, for instance Julio Cortázar's *Rayuela* (1966), in which the topology is multicursal. In yet others, such as Vladimir Nabokov's *Pale Fire* (1962), it may be described as both unicursal and multicursal.

The footnote is a typical example of a structure that can be seen as both uni- and multicursal. It creates a bivium, or choice of expansion, but should we decide to take this path (reading the footnote), the footnote itself returns us to the main track immediately afterward. Perhaps a footnoted text can be described as multicursal on the micro level and unicursal on the macro level. Nabokov's *Pale Fire*, however, leaves the mode of cursality up to the reader; consisting of a foreword, a 999-line poem, a long commentary of notes addressing individual lines (but really telling the commentator's story), and an index, it can be read either unicursally, straight through, or multicursally, by jumping between the comments and the poem. Brian McHale (1987, 18–19) sees it as a limit-text between modernism and postmodernism; it is also a limit-text between uni- and multicursality.

That some texts are hard to define topologically should not surprise us, as it is exactly this aspect of their own ontology they set out to destabilize (cf. McHale 1987, chap. 12). Neither should it discourage us, since the existence of borderline cases and ambiguous structures in no way invalidates the usefulness of categories such as narrative and game or unicursality and multicursality.

The problem is not, finally, that literary critics use words like *labyrinth, game,* and *world* as metaphors in their analyses of unicursal works but that this rhetoric seems to have blinded them to the existence of multicursal literary structures and to the possibility that the concept of labyrinth (in their post-Renaissance rendition) might have more analytic accuracy in connection with texts that function as game-worlds or labyrinths in a literal sense. However, this is not the place to criticize in detail the ontological problems resulting from a possible flaw in the terminology of narrative theory. Such an issue deserves at least a separate study, one not focused on the texts that are our primary concern here. Instead, this might be the place for suggesting the reinstatement of the old dual meaning of *labyrinth,* so that both unicursal and multicursal texts might be examined within the same theoretical framework. With such a theory we might be able to see both how, in Jorge Luis Borges's words, "the book and the labyrinth [are] one and the same" (Borges 1974, 88), and how the many types of literary labyrinths are different from each other. It may surprise some readers to find me still using the word *book,* but a number of the cybertexts we shall discuss are indeed books—printed, bound, and sold in the most traditional fashion. As we shall see, the codex format is one of the most flexible and powerful information tools yet invented, with a capacity for change that is probably not exhausted yet, and I (for one) do not expect it to go out of style any time soon.

Some Examples of Ergodic Literature

At this point it is probably best to liven the discussion with some examples of the literature I am primarily addressing. The exposition made here is mostly for elucidation purposes and must not be mistaken for an attempt to produce an exhaustive historical inventory of ergodic literature (see, instead, Vuillemin 1990). Rather than seeking a catalogue of every known instance of ergodicity, I have focused on diversity. As Roland Barthes (1977, 81) maintains in his study of narrative, it is utopian to examine every specimen of a genre; a deductive method, leading to a "hypothetical model of description," should be applied instead. Thus there may well exist major ergodic genres or texts that I have failed to include, but since this is a theoretical rather than an encyclopedic study, the future appearance of any hitherto unknown forms will invalidate my theories only if they fail to comply with my general model of ergodic forms.

Since writing always has been a spatial activity, it is reasonable to assume that ergodic textuality has been practiced as long as linear writing. For instance, the wall inscriptions of the temples in ancient Egypt were often connected two-dimensionally (on one wall) or three-dimensionally (from wall to wall and from room to room), and this layout allowed a nonlinear arrangement of the religious text in accordance with the symbolic architectural layout of the temple (Gundlach 1985).

Possibly the best-known example of cybertext in antiquity is the Chinese text of oracular wisdom, the *I Ching* (Wilhelm 1989). Also known as the *Book of Changes*, the existing text is from around the time of the Western Chou dynasty (1122–770 b.c.) and was written by several authors. The *I Ching* system also inspired G. W. von Leibniz, who developed the binary mathematics used by today's digital computers (Eber 1979). The *I Ching* is made up of sixty-four symbols, or hexagrams, which are the binary combinations of six whole or broken ("changing") lines ($64 = 2^6$). A hexagram (such as no. 49, ☰ *Ko/Revolution*) contains a main text and six small ones, one for each line. By manipulating three coins or forty-nine yarrow stalks according to a randomizing principle, the texts of two hexagrams are combined, producing one out of 4,096 possible texts. This contains the answer to a question the user has written down in advance (e.g., "How much rice should I plant this year?").

Much simpler examples of nonlinear texts are some of Guillaume Apollinaire's "calligrammes" from early in this century (Apollinaire 1966). The words of these poems are spread out in several directions to form a picture on the page, with no clear sequence in which to be read. A play from the thirties, *Night of January 16th* by Ayn Rand (1936), is about a trial where members of the audience are picked to be the jury. The play has two endings, depending on the jury's verdict. In the early 1960s, Marc Saporta (1962) published *Composition No. 1, Roman,* a novel with pages like a deck of cards, to be shuffled and read in any sequence. It is written in such a way that any combination will appear fluid. (See also Bolter 1991, 140–42.)

A rather well-known example is Raymond Queneau's *Cent Mille Milliards de Poèmes* (a hundred thousand billion poems; see Queneau 1961), which is a sonnet machine book of 10×14 lines, capable of producing 10^{14} sonnets. Several novels have been identified as ergodic over the years: B. S. Johnson's *The Unfortunates* (1969), Milorad Pavic's *Landscape Painted With Tea* (1990), and many others. The variety and ingenuity of devices used in these texts demonstrate that paper can hold its own against the computer as a technology of ergodic texts.

However, after the invention of digital computing in the middle of the twentieth century, it soon became clear that a new textual technology had arrived, potentially more flexible and powerful than any preceding medium. Digital systems for information storage and retrieval, popularly known as databases, signified new ways of using textual material. The database is in principle similar to the filing cabinet but with a level of automation and speed that made radically different textual practices possible. On the physical level, the surface of reading was divorced from the stored information. For the first time, this breaks down concepts such as "the text itself" into two independent technological levels: the interface and the storage medium. On the social level, huge texts could be browsed, searched, and updated by several people at once, and from different places on the globe, operations that only superficially seem to resemble what we used to call "reading" and "writing." Armed with a good search engine and a digital library, any college dropout can pass for a learned scholar, quoting the classics without having read any of them.

Several new textual genres have emerged with digital computing and automation. Computer programs, complex lists of formal instructions written in specially designed, artificial languages, can be seen as a new type of the rhetorical figure *apostrophe*, the addressing of inanimate or abstract objects, with the magical difference that it actually provokes a response. Short, simple programs are often linear, but longer programs generally consist of collections of interdependent fragments, with repeating loops, cross-references, and discontinuous "jumps" back and forth between sections. Given the seminatural vocabulary of some modern programing languages, it is not uncommon for programers to write poems in them, often with the constraint that the "poegrams" (or whatever) must make sense to the machine as well.[1]

Programs are normally written with two kinds of receivers in mind: the machines and other programers. This gives rise to a double standard of aesthetics, often in conflict: efficiency and clarity. Since speed is a major quality in computer aesthetics, an unreadable program might perform much faster than a comprehensible one. The poetics of computer program writing is constantly evolving, and through paradigms such as object orientation it inspires practical philosophies and provides hermeneutic models for organizing and understanding the world, both directly (through programed systems) and indirectly (through the worldviews of computer engineers).

Through the artificial intelligence research of the sixties, programs emerged that one could "talk" to. The best known of these is

---

1. For an example of this type of poetry, not to be confused with computer-generated poetry, see Sharon Hopkins' poem "Listen" (Hopkins 1995), written in the computer-programing language Perl.

Eliza, made in 1963 by an MIT computer scientist, Joseph Weizenbaum. Eliza could imitate a Rogerian psychoanalyst, and through a simple pattern-matching algorithm, it used the information given by its human "clients" to make them believe that it somehow "understood" their situations. Another seminal program, and one of the key texts in this study, is the role-playing game *Adventure*, by William Crowther and Don Woods, released on the U.S. research network ARPANET, the precursor of the Internet, in April 1976.[2] As the microcomputer home market exploded around 1980, *Adventure* was made available on nearly every type of machine and became the first in a short-lived, but influential, textual computer game genre, which ended its commercial life when the graphic adventure games took over in the late eighties.

In the seventies, some artificial intelligence researchers focused on making systems that could analyze and write stories. A well-known project was James Meehan's program Tale-spin, which could construct simple animal fables of the Æsop type. Primarily, the researchers were not trying to achieve literary quality, and the stories that were produced typically testify to this lack of ambition. However, some of the "failures" produced by Tale-spin make strikingly original prose, succeeding where the successes failed. A later system, the commercial dialogue program Racter, created by William Chamberlain (1984), is even supposed to have written a book, *The Policeman's Beard Is Half Constructed*, but as it turns out, the book was co-written (at least) by Chamberlain (see Barger 1993 and chapter 6, below). Although the output of these generators are linear stories or poems, the systems themselves are clearly ergodic textual machines, with unlimited possibility for variation.

Another type of digital ergodic text was conceived by the American Ted Nelson around 1965 (Nelson 1965; see also Nelson 1987). Nelson called this *hypertext*, a strategy for organizing textual fragments in an intuitive and informal way, with "links" between related sections of a text or between related parts of different texts in

2. Personal correspondence with Woods, by E-mail, dated September 29, 1993. I am grateful for his illuminating reply and for the fabulous computer network that makes the Homers of digital literary history still available to researchers.

the same retrieval system. Hypertext has gained in popularity in the last decade, after personal computer programs such as Hypercard were made available and educators started to take an interest in its pedagogical potential. At the same time, literary authors started to experiment with hypertext and have received considerable attention from literary circles. Hyperfictions such as Michael Joyce's *Afternoon: A Story* (1990) engage a modernist poetics to subvert traditional storytelling and present a literary labyrinth for the reader to explore.

In 1980, inspired by William Crowther and Don Woods' *Adventure* (1976), two English programmers at the University of Essex, Roy Trubshaw and Richard Bartle, constructed an adventure game that several players could play at once (see Bartle and Trubshaw 1980; Bartle 1984). They called their invention *Multi-User Dungeon* (*MUD*, also known as *MUD1*), and soon participants from many parts of the world phoned in from their modems to the Essex computer to participate in the new social reality. The first MUDs were oriented toward game playing and puzzle solving, but later MUDs, such as James Aspnes's 1989 *TinyMUD*, allowed users to build their own textual objects and landscapes, and soon the users came to regard themselves as participants in a community, rather than a game, with communication rather than competition as the main social activity. As literature (although not as textual media), MUDs are very different from anything else, with their streams of continuing text and their collective, often anonymous readership and writership. Life in the MUD is literary, relying on purely textual strategies, and it therefore provides a unique laboratory for the study of textual self-expression and self-creation, themes that are far from marginal in the practice of literary theory.

The Aim of This Study

It is a common belief that the rapid evolution in the field of digital technology from the middle of the twentieth century to the present has (among other equally astounding results) brought on radically new ways of writing and reading. This view, stimulated by the increasing personal experience with computer technology among the academic masses, can be observed even in literary studies, which since 1984 have increasingly attempted to capture and construct computer-mediated texts as objects of literary criticism. The present study can be located both inside and outside of this research. In addition to an analysis—and to some extent a construction—of the perceived objects by means of literary theory, this is a study of the problems of such construction and, hence, a critical study of the strategies used by literary researchers to expand their empirical field in this direction. Especially, I wish to challenge the recurrent practice of applying the theories of literary criticism to a new empirical field, seemingly without any reassessment of the terms and concepts involved. This lack of self-reflection places the research in direct danger of turning the vocabulary of literary theory into a set of unfocused metaphors, rendered useless by a translation that is not perceived as such by its very translators. Thus the interpretations and misinterpretations of the digital media by literary theorists is a recurrent theme of this book.

A related but reverse problem is the tendency to describe the new text media as radically different from the old, with attributes solely determined by the material technology of the medium. In these analyses, technical innovation is presented as a cause of social improvement and political and intellectual liberation, a historical move away from the old repressive media. This kind of technological determinism (the belief that technology is an autonomous force that causes social change) has been refuted eloquently by Langdon Winner (1986), James W. Carey (1988), and others but continues, nevertheless, to dominate the discussion. In the context of literature, this has led to claims that digital technology enables readers to become authors, or at least blurs the (supposedly political) distinction between the two, and that the reader is allowed to create his or her own "story" by "interacting" with "the computer." The ideological forces surrounding new technology produce a rhetoric of novelty, differentiation, and freedom that works to obscure the more profound structural kinships between superficially heterogeneous media. Even the inspiring and perceptive essays of Richard Lanham (1993) are suffused by this binary rhetoric and, ultimately, dominated by politics at the expense of analysis.

Whether concepts such as "computer literature" or "electronic textuality" deserve to be defended theoretically is by no means obvious, and they will not be given axiomatic status in this book. The idea that "the computer" is in itself capable of producing social and historical change is a strangely ahistorical and anthropomorphic misconception, yet it is as popular within literary-cultural studies as it is in the science fiction texts they sometimes study. Often, in fact, science fiction portrays the technology with an irony that the critical studies lack (see, e.g., William Gibson's short story, "Burning Chrome," in Gibson 1986).

Most literary theories take their object medium as a given, in spite of the blatant historical differences between, for instance, oral and written literature. The written, or rather the printed, text has been the privileged form, and the potentially disruptive effects of media transitions have seldom been an issue, unlike semantic transitions such as language translation or intertextual practices. At this point, in the age of the dual ontology of everyday textuality (screen or paper), this ideological blindness is no longer possible, and so we have to ask an old question in a new context: What is a text? In a limited space such as this, it is impossible to recapture the arguments of previous discussions of this question. And since the empirical basis for this study is different from the one assumed in these discussions, the arguments would be of limited value. In the context of this study, the question of the text becomes a question of verbal media and their functional differences (what role does a medium play?), and only subsequently a question of semantics, influence, otherness, mental events, intentionality, and so forth. These philosophical problems have not left us, but they belong to a different level of textuality. In order to deal with these issues responsibly, we must first construct a map of the new area in which we want to study them, a *textonomy* (the study of textual media) to provide the playing ground of *textology* (the study of textual meaning).

The production of new maps, however, is also a construction of "newness," whose political consequences we cannot hope to escape. The field of literary study is in a state of permanent civil war with regard to what constitutes its valid objects. What right have we to export this war to foreign continents? Even if important insights can be gained from the study of extraliterary phenomena with the instruments of literary theory (cautiously used), it does not follow that these phenomena are literature and should be judged with literary criteria or that the field of literature should be expanded to include them. In my view, there is nothing to be gained from this sort of theoretical imperialism, but much to lose: discussions of the "literariness" of this or that verbal medium are ever in danger of deteriorating into a battle of apologetic claims and chauvinistic counterclaims. When much energy is spent on showing that P is a perfectly deserving type of Q, the more fundamental question of what P is will often be neglected. These nonproductive (and nonacademic) campaigns in favor of marginal media or aesthetic forms of expression are pathetic signs of a larger problem, however: they illustrate only too well the partial and conservative state of the human sciences, in which nothing can be studied that is not already within a field; in which the type rather than the individual qualities of an object determines its value as an accepted member of some canon or other. Where humanistic study used to be genre chauvinistic, it is now medium chauvinistic, organized into empirical fields (literature, art history, theater, mass communication) with not enough concern for general or intermediary perspectives. This "empirical" partitioning is of course unempirical in consequence, since it excludes empirical material that does not belong to the sanctioned sectors. Also, the limited view privileged by this sort of specializing tends to produce apologetics disguised as criticism, in an age where the "inherent" quality of literature (or any other previously dominant mode of discourse) is no longer self-evident.

Strangely, the struggle between the proponents and opponents of "digital literature" deteriorates usually on both sides into material arguments of a peculiar fetishist nature. One side focuses on the exotic hardware of the shiny new technologies, like CD-ROM. Witness especially the computer industry slogan, "information at your fingertips," as if information were somehow a touchable object. The other side focuses on the well-known hardware of the old technology, the "look and feel" of a book, compared to the crude letters on a computer screen. "You can't take it to bed with you" is the sensuous (but no longer true) refrain of the book chauvinists.

Isn't the content of a text more important than these materialistic, almost ergonomic, concerns?

What these strangely irrelevant exuberances reveal, I think, is that beyond the obvious differences of appearance, the real difference between paper texts and computer texts is not very clear. Does a difference even exist? Instead of searching for a structural divide, this study begins with the premise that no such essential difference is presumed. If it exists, it must be described in functional, rather than material or historical, terms. The alternative, to propose an essential difference and then proceed to describe it, does not allow for the possibility that it does not exist and is, therefore, not an option. Whether it exists or not is not of great importance to this thesis, however, as such knowledge would not make much practical difference in the world. The emerging new media technologies are not important in themselves, nor as alternatives to older media, but should be studied for what they can tell us about the principles and evolution of human communication.

My main effort is, therefore, to show what the functional differences and similarities among the various textual media imply about the theories and practices of literature. The exploration is based on the concepts and perspectives of narratology and rhetoric but is not limited to these two disciplines. I argue that existing literary theory is incomplete (but not irrelevant) when it comes to describing some of the phenomena studied here, and I try to show why and where a new theoretical approach is needed. My final aim is to produce a framework for a theory of cybertext or ergodic literature and to identify the key elements for this perspective.

What Is Cybertext?

In the current discussions of "computer literacy," hypertext, "electronic language," and so on, there seems to emerge an explicit distinction between the printed, or paper-based, text and the electronic text, both with singular and remarkably opposing qualities. The arguments for this distinction are sometimes historical, sometimes technological, but eminently political; that is, they don't focus on what these textual genres or modes are but on their assumed functional difference from each other. Such a strategy is useful for drawing attention to, but less so for the analysis of, the objects thus constructed. It might have been tempting to follow this rhetoric in my investigation of the concept of cybertext and to describe a dichotomy between it and traditional, conventional literature; but the meaning of these concepts is unstable to the point of incoherence, and my construct would therefore probably have reached a similar degree of uselessness.

Cybertext, then, is not a "new," "revolutionary" form of text, with capabilities only made possible through the invention of the digital computer. Neither is it a radical break with old-fashioned textuality, although it would be easy to make it appear so. Cybertext is a *perspective* on all forms of textuality, a way to expand the scope of literary studies to include phenomena that today are perceived as outside of, or marginalized by, the field of literature—or even in opposition to it, for (as I make clear later) purely extraneous reasons. In this study I investigate the literary behavior of certain types of textual phenomena and try to construct a model of textual communication that will accommodate any type of text. This project is not as ambitious as it might sound, since the model is provisional and empirical and subject to future modification should any "falsificatory" evidence (such as an unpredictable object) appear. This pragmatic model is presented in detail in chapter 3.

The rest of this introductory chapter discusses the conceptual foundations and implications of this approach and establishes the terminology applied in the analytical chapters. These chapters (4 through 7) each takes on a main category (or genre) of cybertext roughly corresponding to the results of the analysis in chapter 3: hypertext, the textual adventure game, computer-generated narrative and participatory world-simulation systems, and the social-textual MUDs of the global computer networks. This pragmatic partitioning, which derives from popular convention rather than from my own theoretical model, is motivated by my strong belief that, in such a newly awakened field, theoretical restraint is imperative. Theories of literature have a powerful ability to co-opt new fields and fill theoretical vacuums, and in such a process of colonization, where the "virgin territory" lacks theoretical defense, important perspectives and insights might be lost or at least overlooked. When we invade foreign ground, the least we can do is to try to learn the native language and study the local customs. Although several studies have already been carried out within most of these subfields, almost none have produced overarching, or universal, perspectives or engaged in a comparative analysis of all the forms of textuality examined here. Therefore, these previous approaches are discussed in their respective chapters rather than in this general introduction.

Because there are strong similarities between new and old types of ergodic literature, "the computer" and "information technology" as such will not be an explaining factor in this study but, instead, part of the field to be explored. This approach frees us from trying to define such vague and unfocused terms as *digital text* or *electronic literature* and allows us to develop a function-oriented perspective, in which the rhetoric of media chauvinisms will have minimal effect on the analysis. To be sure, media are far from neutral, inconsequential carriers of "content," but the essentialist idea of "the computer medium" as a singular structure of well-defined properties of communication is just as untenable and can be based on only a very limited understanding of both computer applications and media theory. Computer technology can sustain many different types of media, with very distinctive characteristics. Such a pluralist perspective will help us avoid the traps of technological determinism and let us see the technology as an ongoing process of, rather than a cause of, human expression. As we shall see, many of the forms of computer-based textuality have more in common with some of the paper media than with each other.

As can be inferred from its etymology, a cybertext must contain some kind of information feedback loop. In one sense, this holds true for any textual situation, granted that the "text" is something more than just marks upon a surface. A reader peruses a string of words, and depending on the reader's subsequent actions, the significance of those words may be changed, if only imperceptibly. The act of rereading is a crucial example: the second time we read a text, it is different, or so it seems. How can we know the text from the reading? Sometimes, a reader may influence the text for other readers, even if all the "marks on the pages" stay the same: a dramatic example is the ayatollah Khomeiny's reaction to *The Satanic Verses*. The conventional split between text and reading (between the "intentional object" and the "mental event"), or *signifiant* and *signifié*, is not an impermeable membrane: leaks occur constantly; through various stages of reception such as editing, marketing, translation, criticism, rediscovery, canonization, or banishment.

These well-known processes are not entirely trivial, however, because they remind us that a text can never be reduced to a stand-alone sequence of words. There will always be context, convention, contamination; sociohistorical mediation in one form or another. Distinguishing between a text and its readings is not only necessary, it is also quite impossible—an ideal, in other words. On the one hand we need the image of "the text" in order to focus on anything at all; on the other hand we use the metaphor of "reading" to signal that our apprehension of a text will always be partial, that we never quite reach the "text itself," a realization that has led certain critics to question the very existence of such an object (see, for instance, Fish 1980). This hermeneutic movement or desire—perhaps better described as asymptotic than circular—holds true for all kinds of textual communication, but the particular organization of a text can make both the reader's strategic approach and the text's perceived teleology very distinctive, perhaps to the point where interpretation is stretched beyond the cognitive bounds of a singular concept. It is this field of varying textual organization that this study attempts to clarify. The differences in teleological orientation—the different ways in which the reader is invited to "complete" a text—and the texts' various self-manipulating devices are what the concept of cybertext is about. Until these practices are identified and examined, a significant part of the question of interpretation must go unanswered.

The meaning of *text* used in this study is closer to philological (or observable) work than to the poststructural (or metaphysical) galaxy of signifiers. But though my meaning is related to both of these meanings, it is also radically different from them. Instead of defining *text* as a chain of signifiers, as linguists and semioticians do, I use the word for a whole range of phenomena, from short poems

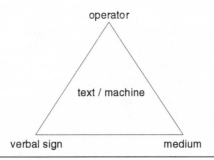

Figure 1.1. The Textual Machine

to complex computer programs and databases. As the *cyber* prefix indicates, the text is seen as a machine—not metaphorically but as a mechanical device for the production and consumption of verbal signs. Just as a film is useless without a projector and a screen, so a text must consist of a material medium as well as a collection of words. The machine, of course, is not complete without a third party, the (human) operator, and it is within this triad that the text takes place. (See figure 1.1.) The boundaries between these three elements are not clear but fluid and transgressive, and each part can be defined only in terms of the other two. Furthermore, the functional possibilities of each element combine with those of the two others to produce a large number of actual text types.

Previous models of textuality have not taken this performative aspect into account and tend to ignore the medium end of the triangle and all that goes with it. In his phenomenology of literature, Roman Ingarden (1973, 305–13) insists that the integrity of the "literary work of art" depends on the "order of sequence" of its parts; without this linear stability the work would not exist. While Ingarden here certainly acknowledges the importance of the objective shape of the text, he also reduces it to a given.

This taken-for-grantedness is hardly strange, since it is only after we have started to notice the "medium" and its recent shifting appearances that we can begin to observe the effect this instability has on the rest of the triangle. As Richard Lanham (1989, 270) observes, literary theorists have for a long time been in the "codex book business," restricting their observations (but not their arguments) to literature mediated in a certain way. Even within the field of codex literature there is room, as experimentalists from Laurence Sterne to Milorad Pavic have demonstrated, for mediational variation, but these attempts have not, apparently, produced sufficient contrast to provoke a systematic investigation of the aesthetic role of the medium (a notable but much too brief exception being McHale 1987, chap. 12). There is also the fascinating phenomenon known as "Artists' Books," an art movement that originated in the sixties and dedicated to the creation of unique works of art that challenge the presumed properties of the book from within (cf. Strand 1992b and Lyons 1985).

Cybertext, as now should be clear, is the wide range (or perspective) of possible textualities seen as a typology of machines, as various kinds of literary communication systems where the functional differences among the mechanical parts play a defining role in determining the aesthetic process. Each type of text can be positioned in this multidimensional field according to its functional capabilities, as we shall see in chapter 3. As a theoretical perspective, cybertext shifts the focus from the traditional threesome of author/sender, text/message, and reader/receiver to the cybernetic intercourse between the various part(icipant)s in the textual machine. In doing so, it relocates attention to some traditionally remote parts of the textual galaxy, while leaving most of the luminous clusters in the central areas alone. This should not be seen as a call for a renegotiation of "literary" values, since most of the texts drawn attention to here are not well suited for entry into the competition for literary canonization.

The rules of that game could no doubt change, but the present work is not (consciously, at least) an effort to contribute to the hegemonic worship of "great texts." The reason for this is pragmatic rather than ethical: a search for traditional literary values in texts that are neither intended nor structured as literature will only obscure the unique aspects of these texts and transform a formal investigation into an apologetic crusade. If these texts redefine literature by expanding our notion of it—and I believe that they do—then they must also redefine what is literary, and therefore they cannot be measured by an old, unmodified aesthetics. I do not believe it is possible to avoid the influence from literary theory's ordinary business, but we should at least try to be aware of its strong magnetic field as we approach the whiter spaces—the current final frontiers—of textuality.

The question of how to approach theoretically the empirical field implied in the term *cybertext* is a hard one. I have suggested that cybertext is more of a perspective on textuality than a category of it; but like all perspectives, it will necessarily emphasize certain types of text and marginalize others. Fundamentally, the answer becomes a definition of textuality in addition, rather than in opposition, to previous definitions such as the philological, phenomenological, structural, semiotic, and poststructural concepts of text, to mention a few. So why not use one of these approaches, instead of concocting a new (and most likely idiosyncratic) one? Simply because none of these have expressed the perspective of the text as a material machine, a device capable of manipulating itself as well as the reader. The various effects produced by cybertextual machines are not easily described by these textological epistemes, if they can be described at all. I might achieve something by trying each one, but since all of them so obviously conceive the material, historical, and textual artifact as a syntagmatic chain of signifiers and little else, that approach would most likely prove fruitless and desultory, and it would almost certainly not illuminate the idiomatic aspects of ergodic texts.

Problems in Computer Semiotics

Even semiotics, the most materially oriented of these epistemes, does not seem to offer any readily useful perspectives in this context. Per Aage Brandt notes that "neither the interpretative semiotics based on the Peircean tradition (such as Eco 1976), nor the structural semiotics of the Saussurean tradition (such as Greimas 1976)—though both are necessary—seem sufficient to follow up the substantial change induced by the on-going implementation of these machines in our 'life world,' probably for the very simple reason that even these often rather sophisticated semiotic elaborations fail to see what a 'symbolic machine' actually is and what it can do" (1993, 128).

Brandt's sensitive and candid critique (coming as it does from within the semiotic field) nevertheless trivializes the reason for recent semiotic theory's inability to account for cybernetic sign production, since these phenomena could not have been invisible to theoreticians such as Umberto Eco and A. J. Greimas, who surely (in Eco's case, evidently; see Eco 1994, 1–2) must have had some contact with the cybernetic ideas and experiments of contemporary individuals and groups such as Raymond Queneau (1961), Italo Calvino (1993), and Ouvroir de Littérature Potentielle (OuLiPo 1981). If these phenomena, together with computer machinery and principles in general, were indeed invisible to the semioticians of that time, then I suggest that the reason for this blind spot is to be found in the semiological paradigm (which seems inherently unable to accommodate the challenge from cybernetic sign systems) and not in the lack of historical opportunity.

Not all proponents of semiotics share Brandt's restraint. J. David Bolter (1991) claims that "the theory of semiotics becomes obvious, almost trivially true, in the computer medium" (196), but this seems to be based on a misreading of the semiotic (specifically, C. S. Peirce's) notion of sign.[1] As Allen Renear (1995, 308) points out, Bolter does not support his claim with substantial analysis and argument. As we shall see, however, even much more modest claims about the relationship between computer technology and semiotics become problematic when put under closer scrutiny. Bolter's assertion must be read in light of the larger project within the hypertext community of trying to connect their technology-ideology of hypertext to various paradigms of textual theory, as "embodiments"

---

1. Compare J. David Bolter: "In a printed dictionary, we must move from page to page, looking up definitions, if we are to set in motion the play of signs" (1991a, 198). Bolter equates the mechanical processing of a hypertext link with what "takes place in our heads" and sees both phenomena as "acts of interpretation." He also claims that "in Peirce's terms, the computer system itself becomes the interpretant for each sign" (199). In Peirce's terms, perhaps, but not in any legitimate interpretation of his concepts.

and "incarnations"—in this case, for Bolter, "the embodiment of semiotic views of language and communication" (1991, 195). Behind all this, of course, lies the age-old dream of a technology that maps onto the workings of the mind, and here, at least, hypertext ideology and semiotics may have some common ground. These problems and issues cannot be fully addressed here, however, as our concern with semiotics must be limited to an investigation of whether it can provide a viable theoretical foundation for the study of cybernetic textuality.

For semiotics, as for linguistics, texts are chains of signs and, therefore, linear by definition (Hjelmslev 1961, 30). As Tomás Maldonado (1993, 58–66) argues in his excellent essay on virtual reality, semiotics (with particular reference to the work of A. J. Greimas) has not managed to meet the challenge from "a whole typology of iconic constructions, very different from those studied by semiotics until now."[2] The new constructions consist of "interactive dynamic" elements, a fact that renders traditional semiotic models and terminology, which were developed for objects that are mostly static, useless in their present, unmodified form. Maldonado's critique concerns the analysis of visual images, but it is equally relevant in the case of ergodic textuality, where the same difference applies.

To be sure, efforts to describe cybernetic systems in terms of semiotics have been made. Jens F. Jensen (1990) calls for a "computer semiotics" as the potentially most effective paradigm for "formatting" the field of "computer culture" studies (12). It is easy to agree with Jensen that the humanistic study of information technological artifacts is characterized by a "theoretical, methodological and conceptual heterogeneity and inconsistency" (47) at the moment (although this is not necessarily a weakness at this still early stage of research), but his statement that this area of study is "basically and primarily a semiotic domain" (47) is much less self-evident. In his effort to claim the field for semiotics, he makes a number of assertions like "the computer is a *semiotic* machine" (47), "programs and data are representations, signs, symbols" (46), and "the computer is a medium that is based on signs as communication" (48). We should

2. The English translations of Maldonado and Jensen that follow are my own.

then reasonably expect a definition of *sign* that will support his claim (and answer Maldonado's challenge), but this is not offered by Jensen. Instead, he offers an elaboration of Eco's discussion (1976) of the "lower threshold" between semiotics and the signals of information theory, which is interesting but ultimately disappointing, since it presupposes a dichotomy between semiosis (the process whereby signs are interpreted and translated into other signs) and information processing in which the latter must be considered as falling outside the territory of semiotics. Jensen sees computer programs as representations and models of some aspect of the real world (1990, 44) and, later, argues that "the symbols as strings of binary digits" (46) can only mean what the programmers and system designers by convention have defined them to mean. As the incarnation of the signal-semiotic threshold, Jensen posits the "interface" (47), the visible front layer of the computer, since it functions both as border-line and membrane between the two systems.

As Eco acknowledges (1976, 21), the idea of this threshold is problematic, and it seems to me that it also excludes the possibility that human mental processes could ever be explained in terms of information processing, a strong hypothesis that still remains to be proven. Notwithstanding the problems of artificial intelligence and cognitive science, there are several relevant cybernetic phenomena that question the validity of Jensen's dichotomous model of information processing and semiosis. Fundamentally, the threshold is invalidated along two interrelated dimensions: complexity and autonomy.

When a system is sufficiently complex, it will, by intention, fault, or coincidence, inevitably produce results that could not be predicted even by the system designer. A typical example is a chess program that plays better than its programer. Even if there is no reason to suspect that anything but meaningless operations of shifting zeroes and ones go on inside the programed machine, it nevertheless displays a significant behavior that is not—and in fact could not—be anticipated by its programer, even if it could be claimed that it was "intended." Furthermore, the ability to predict and counter its opponent's strategy is a form of interpretation (we could call it machine interpretation) that involves something (the signal) that stands for something else (the move) giving rise to a third something (an estimation of the opponent's strategy), to put it in Peirce's terms. A semiotician might dismiss the example on the grounds that it could be better classified as a dyadic relationship, in terms of stimulus (signal) and response (countersignal)—and so it could be!—but then the semiotician would have nothing further to say, since the phenomenon has been relegated to below the threshold. On the other hand, a theory of chess programing could then obviously not afford to be semiotic.

Another type of threshold transgression occurs whenever there is a complexity that cannot be reduced to the finite structure of a specific program or machine; in other words, where the whole is greater than the sum of the perceived parts. A typical example here is the notoriously unstable state of global trade networks, in which the buying and selling of shares and currencies are automated to such an extent that prediction and explanation of events are best left to chaos theory. Such a transglobal system is clearly autonomous, since it cannot be controlled, shut down, or restructured by a single organization or even a country. Its machine-human borders are also unclear, since the interface could hide a human trader, a machine, or a cyborg, a combination of both. Such a system, even if it consisted purely of automatic agents, is not a model or a representation of something else; it is itself, a cybernetic entity that communicates with all and answers to no one. Again, the ongoing process might be described as semiosis, an endless reinterpretation of triadic signs (such as a share, its value, and the implied status of the corresponding company). Perhaps a semiotician watching two unknown trading entities through a stock exchange terminal would still insist that "while people participate in *semiosis*, machines participate in *information processing*" (Jensen 1990, 36), but this perspective would not make any difference to the reality of the symbolic exchange, nor would it be sufficient to specify the cybernetic nature of the participants.

Yet another example would be self-replicating computer "viruses" that spread autonomously from machine to machine and that, in some cases, are programed to mutate their own "anatomy" to avoid detection by antivirus programs. Since their chances for survival depend on their success in transforming themselves to unrecognizability, their resulting semiotic shape is not the direct result of human sign construction but a product refined by an uncontrolled process of "natural selection." However, the question of whether or not the above examples can be said to imply semiosis seems to me ultimately inconsequential, since their deep structures, accessible to us in a way mental processes (at present) are not, must be studied and catalogued if we are to make any sense of the surface signs to which they give rise. To find a name for these sign mechanisms should not be an essential issue. Perhaps we can follow Thomas A. Sebeok's suggestion and develop a notion of "cybersemiosis," agreeing, as he does, with C. S. Peirce that "the essential nature and fundamental varieties of possible semiosis . . . need not be a mental mode of being" (quoted in Sebeok 1991, 99).[3]

Jensen's decision to posit the interface as a border between human semiosis and machine processing, on the other hand, makes it hard to see what relevance a semiotic approach and the idea of semiosis can have in the study of sign-producing machines. As the examples above and the story generators discussed in chapter 6 should indicate, the quasi-autonomous nature of complex sign machines makes a behavioral study of surface sign phenomena rather inadequate and unsatisfactory. These constructs are not simply media by which a human programer communicates with human receivers; they are also comments on such communication: aesthetic or pragmatic modes for the exploration of sign production. (Of course, one could counterclaim that the programers are the media through which these structures reproduce themselves. Both claims are equally uninteresting, as they tell us nothing about the principles of the cybernetic production of signs.)

The crucial issue here is how to view systems that feature what is known as emergent behavior, systems that are complex structures evolving unpredictably from an initial set of simple elements. The science that studies such phenomena is sometimes called "artificial

3. As it happened, Peirce formulated the idea of using electrical circuits instead of mechanical ones to form the "logic gates" (AND, OR, NOT, etc.) of modern computers in 1886, almost sixty years before computers using this technology were constructed (see Burks 1986, 10–15, 42–45).

Figure 2.1. Two Stages of a Glider Gun in John Conway's *Game of Life*

life" and uses computers to build artificial, autonomous "worlds" based on biological principles. The objects they focus on are mathematical constructs known as cellular automata, originally described by computer pioneer John Von Neumann (see Levy 1992). The best-known example is probably John Conway's *Game of Life*, which is a simple two-dimensional grid of cellular automata in which each position, or cell, can be in one of two states: on (alive) or off (dead). Over time, a cell will survive if it is surrounded by two or three others, it will be born if it is an empty cell surrounded by exactly three others, or it will die if it is either overcrowded (surrounded by more than three others) or isolated (surrounded by less than two others). From a random and chaotic initial state, after a few generations the life grid will display orderly patterns and is able to produce complex, multicelled structures with interesting, dynamic behavior.

In figure 2.1 we see the famous glider gun, a self-organized machine that periodically produces offspring (the "gliders" escaping upward to the left). These systems are not models or representations of something else but, rather, evolving, self-organizing entities whose behavior cannot be described as the sign production of a human programer. It would be wrong to classify them as simulations (dynamic models that mimic some aspects of a complex process), since there does not have to be any external phenomenon they can be said to simulate. The fundamental question, however, is whether a system capable of producing emergent behavior based on an initial state and a set of generative rules should be considered a semiotic system at all. Since it can exist without any semiotic output, as a closed process running inside a computer, the semiotic aspect is clearly arbitrary and secondary to the process itself. To the researcher, the semiotic aspect is indispensable as a front end, a practical means to observe and gain knowledge of the evolutionary process going on inside, but this does not imply that the process is basically a semiotic one or that the studied object should be classified as a sign, only that the activity of observation by necessity has to involve a semiotic system of some sort.

If we turn to systems designed primarily to construct a readable sign or message, such as a story generator, the problem is less easily resolved. The behavior of such a system could still be emergent, for instance if the generated story contained a totally unexpected narrative figure, but the teleology of this behavior is undoubtedly semiotic, even if its intrinsic principles are identical to those of other cellular automata.

The idea that cybernetic sign systems are basically mouthpieces for their human designers and programers can also be found in Peter Bøgh Andersen (1990, 137). Andersen's effort to examine computer communication from within a semiotic episteme is a comprehensive study of computer systems from the perspective of Hjelmslevian semiotics; only a small part of it is addressed here. Like Jensen, Andersen uses the interface as the empirical domain for his semiology. In part 2 of his book, he presents a typology of "computer-based signs" derived from his studies of various computer programs, mostly for the Macintosh computer. Chief among his examples are two graphic action games, the classic video arcade game *Breakout*,[4] where the user tries to demolish a "brick wall" by hitting it with a ball steered by a paddle (see ibid., fig. 2.3), and the more advanced and impressive *Dark Castle* (*DC*), created by Jonathan Gay and Mark Stephen Pierce (1986). In *DC*, the player must move a "hero," or user-controlled character ( ), armed with bags of rocks

---

4. The original version of *Breakout* was created by Steve Jobs for Nolan Bushnell's company Atari in the early seventies (see Levy 1984, 263). This game exists in numerous versions and is usually known under the name *Brickles* in its shareware, or public domain, manifestations. I am grateful to Douglas Nonast (personal correspondence) and the Usenet news group rec.games.video.classic for this information.

(🐍), through the obstacles of a dungeon filled with various dangerous traps and enemies, such as poisonous bats (🦇), rats (🐀), or
robot guards (🤖).

Andersen dismisses C. S. Peirce's typology of symbols, indexes,
and icons, since he finds them "not sensitive to the characteristics of computer-based signs, namely that they can be handled and
interacted with" (199). Instead, he sets up his own classification system based on four features: permanence, transience, handling, and
action. These are not independent of each other, however; transience
is subordinate to permanence, and handling is subordinate to action.
By *permanence,* Andersen means the ability of a sign to be recognized throughout its existence. *Transience* is the ability to change
parts of the sign's appearance or context while remaining identifiable as the same sign. *Handling* refers to the user's ability to control
the sign by direct signals, for example, joystick movements. *Action*
refers to the sign's ability to cause changes without the necessary
participation of another sign. From these four features, Andersen
extracts seven classes of signs: interactive, actor, object, button, controller, layout, ghost (table 2.1).

An interactive sign is permanent, transient, active, and can be
handled directly by the user; the hero of *DC* is a good example.
An actor is an active, transient sign that cannot be handled directly,
such as an enemy in *DC*. Objects are inactive and transient, buttons are nontransient but not directly handleable. Controllers (e.g.,
"floors" and "walls" in *DC*) are nontransient, not handleable, but
active. Layout signs are permanent, nontransient, and inactive — in
other words, mere decoration. Last, Andersen posits a very strange
sign indeed; the ghost sign, which is without permanent and transient features, cannot be handled or even perceived but, nevertheless, exists "by influencing the behavior of other non-ghost signs"
(211). The ghost sign is a clear indicator of a main weakness of his
otherwise fairly scrupulous semiology: in order to describe these
phenomena as semiotic entities, he must invent a sign type that
is without manifestation, a sign that seems to be pure content: in
other words, not a sign at all. But what is it? Andersen is aware of
this paradox (197, n. 1) but is clearly not very interested in pursuing

Table 2.1. Classification of Computer-Based Signs

Class	Permanence	Transience	Handling	Activeness
Interactive	+	+	+	+
Actor	+	+	−	+
Object	+	+	−	−
Button	+	−	+	+
Controller	+	−	−	+
Layout	+	−	−	−
Ghost	−	−	−	−

Source: Andersen (1990).

Table 2.2. Classification of Signs from *Dark Castle*

Computer-Based Signs	*Dark Castle* Signs
Interactive	Hero
Actor	🐀 🐍 🦇 etc.
Object	No example
Button	No example
Controller	Walls, floors, ropes, stairs, abysses
Layout	No example
Ghost	Trapdoors (?)

Source: Andersen (1990).

it. The type of influence on other signs that the ghost sign is capable of indicates that we are not dealing with activities that can be fully explained in semiotic terms.

Despite Andersen's considerable and interesting efforts, his typology appears both idiosyncratic and inadequate, even when applied to *Dark Castle,* his own chief example (see table 2.2). A number of signs in *DC* are not mentioned by Andersen: rolling boulders, moving platforms (such as the logs in the underground river and the "floating stones" in the stalactite cave; see ibid., fig. 2.1), the small rocks used by the hero to kill or pacify his enemies, not to mention the rock bags (🛍) found throughout the game. How should these four signs be classified (table 2.3)? All four have permanent

Table 2.3. Some Other Signs from *Dark Castle*

Signs	Permanence	Transience	Handling	Activeness
Rolling boulders	+	+	÷	+
Moving platforms	+	+	÷	+
Small rocks	+	+	+	+
Rock bag	+	÷	+	+

Figure 2.2. Moving Platforms and a Slightly Distressed Hero, *Dark Castle*. *Source:* Gay and Pierce (1986).

features (they are recognizably different from other signs; except for the bags, they are transient (moving across the screen); boulders and platforms cannot be directly handled, whereas bags are picked up and rocks thrown by direct user input; all four influence other signs (the bags by allowing the hero to throw more rocks). So far so good. But when we attempt to position these signs in Andersen's classification (table 2.1), things are not so simple. Boulders and platforms both turn out to be actor signs, which is odd, especially in the case of platforms, considering that they cannot be influenced by other signs (fig. 2.2). The rocks turn out to be interactive signs, which is even stranger, since that posits them in the same class as the hero. (On the other hand, the arrows fired by the guards must be actor signs, with the feature set +++.) Finally, the bags, strangely but not inconceivably, turn out to be buttons.

Intuitively, I would classify boulders, rocks, bags, and arrows as objects and moving platforms as controllers. But that wouldn't really solve anything, since I am not able to argue my choices in a general and systematic way. (I might come up with an alternative classification scheme that would allow such a description, but that is still not the same as a general classification.) On trial here, however, is Andersen's semiotic typology, and when we apply it in a rigorous analysis it clearly shows its limitations. That the hero's rocks should end up in the same class as the hero himself and not classified with the guards' arrows and that the boulders and platforms should have the same profile despite their obvious differences (the hero cannot stand on a boulder, for instance) seem sufficient indications of the inadequacy of the model. Furthermore, that a bag of rocks should be classified as a button is also less than satisfactory, because a button (e.g., as found in the Macintosh interface) should always be reachable (even if unclickable) with the cursor, while a bag in *Dark Castle* might be perched on a hard-to-reach ledge, or behind some monster.

The button illustrates my key objections to Andersen's typology. As a class defined by table 2.1, the button is permanent, non-transient, handleable, and active (i.e., may influence other signs). In other words, a button simply exists, waiting without change or movement to carry out the user's order. However, this definition does not apply to most buttons of real computer systems, where a button (as a type of programable object) can do anything its programing system allows. In *Hypercard*, for instance, a button can be dragged, changed, disabled, highlighted, even made invisible, or placed off the screen. It can also be made to behave according to Andersen's definition, but this is clearly a subset of its abilities. A *Hypercard* button, in fact, can fit any of Andersen's sign categories and still be recognized as a button by its users (fig. 2.3).

A trivial solution to this problem would be to rename the button category, calling it, say, a spot. But rather meaningless distinctions would result from such a change, for example, between *Hypercard* buttons with similar appearance and function but with some trivial

Figure 2.3. Four Phases in the Life Cycle of a Button. From left to right:
(1) under configuration; (2) normal; (3) highlighted; (4) disabled. The fifth
phase, invisible, was not present at the taking of this screen picture.

incongruity, such as highlighting or dimming (disabling). Andersen
acknowledges the impurity of this category, admitting that buttons
may have "rudimentary" transient features (Andersen, Holmquist,
and Jensen 1993, 24) but claims that they are a type of interactive
signs whose "transient features are so simple that they call for a special designation" (Andersen 1990, 201). However, a disabled button
is no longer interactive: it has changed into a layout sign, a transition that, while confluent with Andersen's notions of permanence
and transience, violates his categories of handling and action. The
question, Is it still the same sign? cannot be answered. (And it could
also be argued that a disabled button is more like an actor sign than
a layout sign, since it signifies an inaccessible action.)

In his analysis of *Breakout,* it appears that Andersen does not follow his own typology with sufficient rigor. Here he correctly classi-
fies the paddle as interactive and the ball as actor, but the bricks—
wrongly, I think—as object signs, the type that can be influenced by
but not influence other signs. Since the bricks influence the ball by
changing its direction on impact, they are clearly active. Since they
are not directly handleable, they must be either actors or controllers. So the question is, Are they transient? Here we have a problem,
since the individual brick is not transient (it is either there or not
there), whereas the brick wall seen as a whole is transient (changing
shape at every hit; fig. 2.4).

To solve this problem, we might conclude that the individual
brick is a controller sign and that the wall is an actor sign. (And
it does make sense to see the wall as a kind of sign.) In this case,
then, the wall is an actor composed of controllers. Should we accept this analysis, however, the typology inevitably breaks down,
since the two sign types no longer remain independent as analytical
units. A further problem is that Andersen's definition of controller

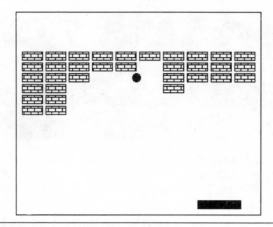

Figure 2.4. The Breakout-type Game *Brickles Plus*.
Source: Winograd (1993).

signs does not allow for the disappearance of a sign in the course of
an action: "controller signs are signs that only change properties of
other objects, not of themselves" (203). Since the bricks disappear
upon impact with the ball, it seems unquestionable that at least one
aspect of the sign—its existence—has changed. However, this aspect is not covered by Andersen's concept of transience, since the
change does not occur during "the lifetime of the sign token" (176).

The most relevant test for a typology of computer-based signs,
however, is to apply it to computer systems other than those discussed in the original proposal. Reasonable criteria for such further
evaluation might be to look at different computer system types
(Andersen's examples in pt. 2, 1.2, seem more or less confined to the
Macintosh system), different discourse types, and especially, inno-
vative systems that might deviate from the types already discussed.

One such system is the game *Lemmings* (Jones, Timmons, and
Johnston 1992). Here the user is in charge of a flock of lemmings and
must steer them through a series of unforgiving landscapes within
a limited time and with as few losses as possible (fig. 2.5). To do this,
the user has only the lemmings themselves, but a limited number of
them can be given certain special functions for a limited period, such
as building stairs, digging through obstacles. By selecting a function

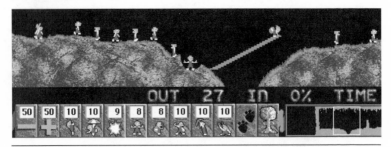

Figure 2.5. A Snapshot from *Lemmings*. *Source:* Jones, Timmons, and Johnston (1992).

from the lower panel on the screen, the player chooses which lemming to endow with which function at which moment. To appoint a special function lemming, the player clicks on the appropriate function button and targets the appropriate lemming with the cursor (which is shaped like the cross hairs of a rifle). The lemming is then transformed from a general purpose lemming (i.e., one that fearlessly marches straight ahead) to a special purpose lemming, which will engage in the special task with equal single-mindedness.

The cursor in *Lemmings* is clearly what Andersen calls an interactive sign: permanent (recognizable), transient (changing), handleable, and active (capable of changing other signs). The lemmings, however, are not so easily classified, since they are both handleable (when transformed by the user) and not handleable (at any other moment). When it comes to action, the special purpose lemming is clearly active, while the standard lemming is incapable of any action except a constant movement straight ahead. (It is even incapable of standing still.) In the standard state, the lemming seems close to being an object sign, since it is incapable of changing anything but its own position. Thus, the lemming is a misfit in Andersen's typology: only transitorily an interactive sign, not quite an object sign, and if an actor sign, then not one but two very different kinds of actor. Finally, the stairs (made by stair-builder lemmings) and the ground (burrowed by digging lemmings) come close to being controller signs, except that, being manipulable (transient), they classify as actor signs instead (table 2.4).

Table 2.4. Some Signs from *Lemmings*

Signs	Permanence	Transience	Handling	Activeness
Cursor	+	+	+	+
Lemming	+	+	(?)	(?)
Stair	+	+	÷	+
Ground	+	+	÷	+

It seems reasonable to conclude that Andersen's typology of computer-based signs is both too elastic and too arbitrary to be really useful in describing systems such as computer games in a rigorous and general way. Objects with distinctly and substantially different features end up in the same category, while objects that are alike do not; yet others seem to belong to several categories with no sound criteria to resolve the matter. But in rejecting Andersen's typology, must we also reject his four basic categories? Two of these categories, permanence and transience, are certainly useful and necessary in identifying and describing signs, but they are not particular to computer contexts. The third, handleability, has proven problematic: where does user action stop and system action begin? The conflict between the user's integrity and the system's autonomy is not confined to the border of the interface; rather it is coded into the behavior of both. Likewise, the fourth category, activeness is open to uncertainty: the idea that a sign (e.g., the ball) is capable of influencing another sign (e.g., the brick) is simply an anthropomorphism. Andersen, of course, knows this but is still unwilling to move his focus on where the real action is: in the mathematical reality beneath the surface, where the relations and objects of the system are being processed.

But, rejecting one semiology, how should we regard other computer semiologies? It would of course be preposterous to reject in advance all semiotic typologies of computer-based communication just because one typology has proven unsuitable to our needs. However, the lessons learned from the experience with one semiology can be generalized and so construed as arguments against the sufficiency of a semiotic approach. The main problem seems to be the assumption that cybernetic sign processes can be understood and classified by observing their surface expressions alone. When the relationship between surface sign and user is all that matters, *the unique dual materiality of the cybernetic sign process is disregarded.* Without an understanding of this duality, however, analyses of communicative phenomena involving cybernetic sign production become superficial and incomplete.

In short, the dual nature of the cybernetic sign process can be described as follows: while some signification systems, such as painted pictures and printed books, exist on only one material level (i.e., the level of paint and canvas, or of ink and paper), others exist on two or more levels, as a book being read aloud (ink-paper *and* voice-soundwaves) or a moving picture being projected (the film strip *and* the image on the silver screen). In these latter cases, the relationship between the two levels may be termed *trivial,* as the transformation from one level to the other (what we might call the secondary sign production) will always be, if not deterministic, then at least dominated by the material authority of the first level. In the cybernetic sign transformation, however, the relationship might be termed *arbitrary,* because the internal, coded level can only be fully experienced by way of the external, expressive level. (When inactive, the program and data of the internal level can of course be studied and described as objects in their own right but not as ontological equivalents of their representations at the external level.) Furthermore, what goes on at the external level can be fully understood only in light of the internal. Both are equally intrinsic, as opposed to the extrinsic status of a performance of a play vis-à-vis the play script. To complicate matters, two different code objects might produce virtually the same expression object, and two different expression objects might result from the same code object under virtually identical circumstances. The possibilities for unique or unintentional sign behavior are endless, which must be bad news for the typologists.

Few critics would attempt to analyze a film adaptation of a novel without studying the novel, yet this seems to be the logical equivalent of a "pure" semiotic approach to computer games and other cyberworks. Just as psychology attempts to explain psychic phenomena without recourse to the existence of ghosts, so the study of cybernetic sign production should attempt to describe its objects without the existence of ghost signs. Also, the existence of a cardinal category of "computer signs" with unique and consistent properties seems doubtful.

I am far from convinced that computer-mediated communication is fundamentally and primarily a semiotic domain, as Jensen claims. But it must be added here that the field of computer semiotics is still very young and that it is far too early to draw any firm conclusions about its viability. However, the problems and shortcomings of the semiotic approaches we have seen so far indicate that semiotics is not beneficial as a *privileged* method of investigation, and it is therefore not pursued with any extraordinary attention in what follows. Instead, due to the lack of any suitable ready-made formalisms, this study is forced into an eclectic and pragmatic approach, which is quite appropriate considering the relatively unexplored nature of our domain. In the rest of this chapter I examine the usefulness of some key concepts to establish a perspective that will facilitate analyses of the categories of cybertext, their aesthetics, construction, and uses.

Textuality, Nonlinearity, and Interactivity

Since the concept of text is heavily contested and unclear already,[5] there should be no real harm done by introducing yet another application of the term (which I define below, in chapter 3). (After all, why should not text, rather than function as a strict category, behave textually—in the Barthesian sense—and rewrite itself at every opportunity?) In a previous essay (Aarseth 1994), I advocated the concept of nonlinear literature, which I defined in the following way: "A nonlinear text is an object of verbal communication that is not simply one fixed sequence of letters, words, and sentences but one in which the words or sequence of words may differ from reading to reading because of the shape, conventions, or mechanisms of the text" (51). Admittedly, this is a very open definition, but not, as some might claim, a purely negatory one. For a text to be nonlinear, it must have a positive distinction: the ability to vary, to produce

5. Compare John Mowitt's (1992) disquisition of text as an "antidisciplinary object."

different courses. As we will see, this distinction manifests itself in many forms and can be described in terms other than the ones I use. Furthermore, these forms relate to the dominant linear form in very different ways—politically, aesthetically, and philologically— so nonlinearity, their common distinction, cannot be described in any of these perspectives. The perspective of nonlinearity therefore is most useful as a starting point, as a means of identifying possible directions; once we arrive, it may not be as useful any more and will have to be replaced by more nuanced analytical tools.

The field produced by the perspective of nonlinearity (with of course linearity included) is not identical to "the field of textuality" (and no one such field is here presumed to exist). Instead, the field produced by the perspective of nonlinearity must be seen as one of many thematizations of textual behavior: writing, literacy, inscription, and so on. Other thematizations, by Jacques Derrida (1976), Walter Ong (1982), David Porush (1985), and many others, are not tangential or contrary enough to warrant extensive commentary here. The issues they address are not paraphrasable by this perspective of nonlinearity, although they can easily be aligned with it on the larger scale of technologizing discourse. Only thematizations that deal with textual machines in a nonmetaphorical sense, such as parts of Eco's "open work," are addressed directly. The line of distinction between metaphorical and actual machines can be defined as the difference between the production of signifieds and the production of signifiers. At some theoretical level this distinction no doubt deconstructs itself (as all texts, as text, produce, stage, and transmaterialize themselves), and we have already seen how unstable the fault line between linear and nonlinear can be within a single text (Vladimir Nabokov's *Pale Fire;* see Nabokov 1962). But the fact that a production of signifiers can go on *within* a (recognized) work without destroying its (epistemological) identity and boundaries strongly suggests the orthodoxy of this perspective. The ideology of "the work," ironically, far from being unzipped by nonlinearity, is hardly challenged by this at all, at a time when other dominant cultural phenomena (parody, digital reproduction, theft and mutation, simulation of all kinds) bear down hard on the notions of integrity, authenticity, territory, and even, to some extent, the market. The only political significance of nonlinearity is that it is in fact apoliti-cal—a perhaps more controversial observation than it might seem.

Martin Rosenberg (1994) reaches a similar position by a differ-ent line of argument in his examination of "the physics tropes that hypertext theorists resort to in order to polemicize the capacity of hypertext to liberate its users" (270). While I agree entirely with his conclusions (see also Moulthrop 1994a), it seems to me that his assumption that *nonlinear* is primarily a trope from physics (and chaos theory) is somewhat overstated. Hypertextual nonlinearity, as an alterity of textual linearity (monosequentiality), can be seen as a topological (rather than tropological) concept, in accordance with the principles of graph theory (cf. Wilson 1983), a concrete phenomenon, defined formally and not metaphorically, in terms of nodes and links (cf. Aarseth 1994, 59). The fact that it can be com-pared to the concept of nonlinearity in physics does not mean that it is derived from that discourse, merely that there is a certain tropo-logical resonance between the two, which, as Rosenberg shows, can be observed in some hypertext theory. In addition to Rosenberg's critique, the terms *nonlinear* and *nonsequential,* originally used by Theodor H. Nelson in his discussions of hypertext (Nelson 1987), have been criticized and partly rejected by other hypertext theo-rists, who suggest the use of *multilinear* and *multisequential* instead (e.g,. Landow 1992a, 4).

Gunnar Liestøl (1994, 103–10) contends that hypertext reading, like all reading, is linear in time and that the act of reading a hyper-text reduces the nonlinearity of space to the linearity of time. But "linearity of time" is a pleonasm and is useless as a categorical de-scription, since there can be no "nonlinearities of time." For Liestøl, *nonlinear* is an "empty term in the discourse on hypermedia, which only shows how preoccupied writers on the subject have been with defining hypermedia in opposition to traditional media" (110). This quite reasonable reprimand is unfortunately somewhat weakened by the pronounced ideological reason for his embrace of *multilinear:* "to stress continuity, relation, and connection rather than negation, difference, and distinction" (110); and it is surprisingly denied by the continued use of "nonlinear" eight pages later as well as by his conclusion that the combination of media types into hypermedia are "simply *different* or *other* than the summation of their preceding elements" (118, his italics). So much, it seems, for continuity.

But what to make of the term *multilinear?* And whose lines are they anyway—the producer's, the work's, or the user's? Clearly, a topology of nodes and links is not linear (or unilinear) if there is more than one possible path between node *A* and node *B*. The question is, then, which of the two terms, *nonlinearity* or *multilinearity*, is better suited to describe such a network. If the paths are simply parallel, never meeting before *B*, then *multilinear* is the natural choice, just as *linear* describes one such path. But if the paths fork, with at most one direct path between any two nodes, as is usually the case in hypermedia, we can no longer talk about paths in any other sense than as a potential path, a course or itinerary. The lines of such a net are not identical to the possible courses, since the same line can occur at different positions in a single course. So, should we decide to use the term *multilinear*, what lines are we referring to, the lines of the net or the lines of the courses? If we refer to the individual lines of the net, the term *multilinear* makes only trivial sense and could, in fact, be wrong, if the whole net can be subsumed under only one line. If we refer to the courses, *multicursal* would be a much more accurate term than *multilinear*, indicating that the lines are produced by movement rather than drawn in advance. But is *nonlinear* better? Can a structure consisting of lines be nonlinear? On the (trivial) level of the line, no; but on the level of the structure as a whole, yes. The sign + is made of two lines, but its form is not linear, as opposed to the signs <, |, or O. If topological shapes are either linear or nonlinear, then hypermedia works, as opposed to hypermedia itineraries, must be topologically nonlinear.

The discrepancy between Nelson and his critics, therefore, can easily be explained: while he is talking of text and writings (as constructed objects), they are talking of readings and writing (as temporal process)—or at least they are not taking that distinction into account. Yet this is a distinction that must be made. Roman Ingarden (1973) dismisses the notion that texts have a temporal dimension:

> Usually one says that the literary and the musical work are both works of "temporal" art . . . and means by that they are *temporally extended*.

As plausible as this may appear at first, it is false, and arises from the confusion of the literary work itself with its concretizations, which are constituted when the work is read. . . . That temporal extension is not an attribute of the literary work itself is already shown by the fact that, if this conception were true, one would have to attribute *different* temporal extensions to one and the same work according to the length of given readings (305–6).

Even if a critic of Ingarden's such as Hans-Georg Gadamer (1989) argues that "the presentation or performance of a work of literature or music is something essential, and not incidental to it" (134), and that "its actual being cannot be detached from its presentation and . . . in this presentation the unity and identity of a structure emerge" (122), because "to be dependent on self-presentation belongs to what it is," then this only amounts to saying that the meeting between work and spectator must take place in a (temporal) reality. Gadamer's ontology of "the work of art" has its own problems, which also are relevant to our discussion of nonlinear literature. Although he emphasizes the importance of seeing the work as a hermeneutic process of change, he still believes in a transcendent and recognizable "work itself" that, "however much it is transformed and distorted . . . still remains itself" (122). Taken to its extreme, this means there can be only one work of art in the world, since any work can be transmuted into any other work or to any imaginable position in between. This is also known as intertextuality, but it is probably not what Gadamer had in mind. Ingarden is much less dogmatic on this issue and asserts that whether "the given concretization can still be considered a concretization of the *same* work, or whether it then expresses an entirely *new* work, is a matter that requires a separate, extensive analysis in each concrete instance" (1973, 340).

We don't have to subscribe to Ingarden's organicist idea of "the work of art as a whole" to recognize that a temporal experience of an object must be different from the object that it is an experience of, if the concepts of *experience* and *object* are to be distinguished from each other at all. Furthermore, since a change in experience does not by necessity imply a change in the object (while it is hard to imagine the opposite being true), the object must be thought of as independent of any particular experience if it is to be thought of at all. We need not think of this object as identical to the "work" but as a material entity that determines it in a way the individual readings (or all of them put together) do not.

In other words, a piece of writing on paper or a computer screen should not be confused with the act of reading it. To say that hypertext readings must be linear is just another way of saying that they are temporal, which again simply refers to the temporality of our existence. It is therefore not valid as an argument against the term *nonlinearity* as used in this context, just as the structure of nonlinearity or multilinearity is not an argument for liberation, as Rosenberg (1994) points out. When we consider these objections to the concept of nonlinearity, we should remember that their context is hypertext and hypermedia, not communication systems in general, and that they are therefore keyed to the special problems facing the hypertext scholar. Other researchers with a more general perspective on textual media might not find the hypertext theorists' perspectives particularly useful—nor the concept of nonlinearity particularly problematic. Thus, Noel Williams (1992, 260), in a discussion of hypertext and adventure games, defines nonlinear text simply as "any text that deviates from the linear paradigm." But what is this linear paradigm?

The gravest objection to the concept of nonlinear textuality is its implied corollary of *linear* textuality. How can a text be linear? Clearly, the physical properties of the codex is not enough to ensure it, as so many paper experiments (e.g., Queneau 1961) have shown. Furthermore, any book can be opened at any page and can be started at any point. The book form, then, is intrinsically neither linear nor nonlinear but, more precisely, random access (to borrow from computer terminology). The book is well suited to linear discourse but is just as accommodating toward nonlinear discourse, as an encyclopedia or a forking-path story. In general, nonlinear text types perform more effectively on a computer system than on paper, but the same can be said of texts whose linear integrity must not be compromised, such as William Gibson's *Agrippa* (Gibson 1992) or the message sculptures of Jenny Holzer (1993). Even hypertext can be a much stronger linear medium than the codex, should its author decide so (cf. Bolter 1991, 125). A hypertext path with only one (unidirectional) link between text chunks is much more authoritarian and limiting than (say) a detective novel, in which the reader is free to read the ending at any time.

To construct a fundamental dichotomy between linear and nonlinear types of media is therefore dangerous; it produces blind spots even as it creates new insights. When we try to use it consistently, linearity turns out to be a treacherous concept. The linearity of Herman Melville's novel *Moby Dick* (1851) is not the same as that of the movie *Gone with the Wind* (1939) nor is it the same when watching the same film on TV or video. As Roland Barthes points out in his comment on *tmesis*, or "skipping" (1975, 10–11), even the most classical narrative carries with it an invitation to discontinuous reading: "a rhythm is established, casual, unconcerned with the *integrity* of the text; our very avidity for knowledge impels us to skim or skip certain passages." This activity of jumping lightly down the page is not marginal but integral to narrative and produces the pleasure of the great narratives: "has anyone ever read Proust, Balzac, *War and Peace*, word for word?" Tmesis, claims Barthes, is not a figure of the text but a figure (at the time) of reading: the author "cannot choose to write *what will not be read.*"

In its current popular use among media theorists, the concept of linearity is at least as ambiguous as that of nonlinearity. Since linearity is not an intrinsic part of the codex structure, we must ascribe its dominance there as primarily an ideological one, perhaps inherited when it succeeded the more strictly linear papyrus scroll as an even more effective way to preserve and represent lengthy texts. The structure of the codex, however, while perfectly suited to linearity, also eased the way for nonlinearity. In that respect, the codex technology is at least as important as the computer in the development of nonlinear textuality. Because of the strong ideological aspects of the linear-nonlinear dichotomy, and because of their rather limited descriptive power, these concepts are not used as defining attributes in the typology presented in the next chapter. Instead, a finer set of criteria is used to describe the various properties and effects usually associated with them.

Another often-used term with strong ideological undercurrents is *interactivity*. This word has long been associated with the use of computers that accept user input while a program is running, as opposed to "batch" computers, which process only preloaded data without interruption. *Interactive* thus came to signify a modern, radically improved technology, usually in relation to an older one. This industrial rhetoric produced concepts such as interactive newspapers, interactive video, interactive television, and even interactive houses, all implying that the role of the consumer had (or would very soon) change for the better. In the computer press, "interactive fiction" made its entrée in a *Byte* article by Bob Liddil (1981), after having been coined by Scott Adams' company, Adventure International (see Buckles 1985, 8). Before that, adventure games were called by many names: storygames, computer fictions, compunovels, among others. Interactive fiction was later introduced to literary studies in an article by Anthony Niesz and Norman Holland (1984). This trajectory is typical of industrial terms appropriated by analysts of technoculture (a more recent example is the ubiquitous "virtual") and shows how commercial rhetoric is accepted uncritically by academics with little concern for precise definitions or implicit ideologies. The word *interactive* operates textually rather than analytically, as it connotes various vague ideas of computer screens, user freedom, and personalized media, while denoting nothing. Its ideological implication, however, is clear enough: that humans and machines are equal partners of communication, caused by nothing more than the machine's simple ability to accept and respond to human input. Once a machine is interactive, the need for human-to-human interaction, sometimes even human action, is viewed as radically diminished, or gone altogether, as in interactive pedagogy. To declare a system interactive is to endorse it with a magic power.

There is of late a growing discontent with the dubiousness of the term, causing researchers in "interactive drama" such as the Oz group at Carnegie Mellon University to call their work "highly interactive" (Kelso, Weyhrauch, and Bates 1992, 1) to distinguish it from other mere "interactive" media such as hypertext. Many hypertext researchers, on the other hand, like to think of interactive fiction as a type of hypertext (cf. Moulthrop 1994b), and this further indicates the ideological character of both these terms as well as the two main positions in the field of "interactive" aesthetics. Formal definitions of interactivity are curiously few, but they do exist. A semiotic definition is given by Peter Bøgh Andersen (1990, 89): "An interactive work is a work where the reader can physically change the discourse in a way that is interpretable and produces meaning within the discourse itself. An interactive work is a work where the reader's interaction is an integrated part of the sign production of the work, in which the interaction is an object-sign indicating the same theme as the other signs, not a meta-sign that indicates the signs of the discourse."

This is an interesting description of the relationship between an adventure game and its player. It is a good description of the normal relationship between a musician and a composition or between a building and its inhabitant. What it describes, however, seems coincidental to the term *interaction* and is perhaps better described as participation, play, or even use. It is not an apt description of a work where the user can contribute discursive elements to the effect that the "theme" of the "discourse itself" is unknown in advance or is subject to change. Nor does it describe discursive systems where the user's activity is limited to metasemiotic exploration. This excludes hypertexts, for example, Michael Joyce's *Afternoon* (Joyce 1990), and does not allow for distinctions between hypertext readers and readers of standard word processing documents. It also seems to deny the possibility of self-reflective works in which metadiscursivity is enacted. Finally, it overlooks the fact that the "reader's interaction" in a typical adventure game "indicates the signs of the discourse" as well as the theme, as when the player is searching for a suitable word to complete a command successfully only to be told by the game's "voice" that it does not understand the word.

Another more socially oriented attempt at defining interactivity, one that strikes much closer to its predigital sense, has been made by Andrew Lippman, who sees it as "mutual and simultaneous activity on the part of both participants, usually working towards some goal, but not necessarily" (quoted in Brand 1988, 46). This is a daring definition, as it implies a functional equality between the interacting agents and a relationship of some sort. Of course, everything hinges on the word "mutual." Defined this way, interactivity between human and machine can take place only if the machine is somehow aware of the situation. This of course conjures up all the problematic issues of artificial intelligence, but for a researcher in artificial intelligence to be working toward interactivity of this kind is only reasonable—and unexceptional. It follows that, by this definition, interactive machines do not yet exist.

What can "interactive fiction" mean, and what does it imply for the meaning and theory of fiction? Since it is used repeatedly without clarification,[6] there can be two possibilities: either it means nothing in particular or its meaning is perceived to be so trivial that it is self-explanatory. The concept of fiction is also curiously under-defined in modern literary theory and barely mentioned in text-books, in which one would expect it to undergo a thorough treatment. It is not hard, on the other hand, to come up with dictionary definitions: a fiction is a representation of an unreal event or object; something invented or imaginary; a lie. In terms of literature, a fiction is a portrayal of invented events or characters, usually in the form of prose (short stories, novels, etc.), constructed in a way that invites rather than dispels belief. A successful fiction must, therefore, in one sense be interactive, just as a lie needs a believer in order to work.

This mutual construction of fiction as an interactive object, however, is intrinsic to narrative literature but is less so to forms such as poetry and drama, which are not usually thought of as fiction. This alone should make us suspicious. Such interactive fiction as an adventure game is even less fictive than a staged drama, since the user can explore the simulated world and establish causal relationships between the encountered objects in a way denied to the readers of *Moby Dick* or the audience of *Ghosts*. The adventure game user cannot rely on imagination (and previous experience) alone but must deduce the nonfictive laws of the simulated world by trial and error in order to complete the game. And a fiction that must be tested to be consumed is no longer a pure fiction; it is a construction of a dif-

6. Compare Anthony Niesz and Norman Holland (1984), Mary Ann Buckles (1985), Neil Randall (1988), Richard Ziegfeld (1989), Sarah Jane Sloane (1991), and Robert Kelley (1993), none of whom explains in what sense interactive fiction is fiction; that is, how the properties of fiction can be said to exist in the works they call interactive.

ferent kind. This empirical dimension makes ergodic works of the adventure game variety stand out from other types of literature and renders the term *interactive fiction* meaningless in this context. It is a purely ideological term, projecting an unfocused fantasy rather than a concept of any analytical substance. This should be sufficient reason for theorists not to use it, although given its popularity, it will probably not go away for a while. Be that as it may, interactive fiction is perhaps best understood as a fiction: the fiction of inter-activity.

Cyborg Aesthetics and the "Work in Movement"

The task of proposing an aesthetic theory for ergodic works, with all their double (both individual and generic) possibilities for varia-tion, is daunting. So many different views and approaches may be found, so many types of literary games and experiments exist, that to construct a continuous field out of these heterogeneous efforts and positions is to exclude much more than can be included. Even so, an important purpose of an aesthetic theory must be to exam-ine the viability of its own perspective. Here I develop the concept of cyborg aesthetics, discussing it in light of John Cayley's ergo-dic *Book Unbound* (1995a). But the first step is of course to discuss earlier approaches.

Perhaps the only major aesthetic theory that directly engages the same types of text as the ergodic perspective can be found in Umberto Eco's 1962 work *Opera Aperta* (see Eco 1989). Here, Eco develops a dichotomy between "open" and "closed" works: works with several plausible interpretations contra works with only one plausible interpretation. The well-known central problems and the ensuing debate need not concern us now, however; they belong to the field of modernist poetics. But as a special subcategory of the open work, Eco describes " 'works in movement,' because they con-sist of unplanned or physically incomplete structural units" (12); and this is exactly the same type of phenomenon that we are addressing here, although within a significantly broader perspective than his. (Some cybertexts do use randomness, and many contain structures that need to be "filled in," or arranged by the user, but the ergodic work is not limited to these means of variation.) Also, his emphasis on the role of the reader shows the main interest to be on the interpretation rather than on the construction of the work. However, Eco's theory remains the only aesthetics (as opposed to poetics, of which there are numerous examples)[7] that foregrounds the general topic of variable expression in works of art.

Eco starts out with four examples of musical "works in movement" (by Stockhausen, Berio, Pousseur, Boulez) and declares that these contemporary pieces, in which the performer must choose a sequence from several alternatives, are " 'open' in a far more tangible sense" (1989, 4) than standard works of art, especially the "time-honored tradition of the classics" (2). (Here, Eco appears to be unaware of Mozart's aleatory minuets, which use a similar principle of performer-induced recombination.) One might then expect a similar emphasis on the literary works in movement, but Eco instead shifts his interest from the combinatorics of signifiers to the combinatorics of signifieds and brings in the "open" poetics of Verlaine, Kafka, Brecht, and above all James Joyce. Comparing the two forms of "openness," he cautions that "none of this argument should be conceived as passing an aesthetic judgment on the relative validity of the various types of works under consideration" (12). But in his few discussions of literary "works in movement," it is hard to see that he is doing anything else. Commenting on Mallarmé's (both biographically and "openly") unfinished *Livre*, Eco expresses doubt that the work would have had any "real value" had it been completed. In a later chapter, we find this rejection of Marc Saporta's (1962) work:

> I recently came across *Composition No. 1*, by Max [sic] Saporta. A brief look at the book was enough to tell me what its mechanism was, and what vision of life (and, obviously, what vision of literature) it proposed, after which I did not feel the slightest desire to read even one of its loose pages, despite its promise to yield a different story every time

7. A poetics, as a more or less formal description of the rules that determine the production of a literary work, can be inferred from, and often be seen to explicitly accompany, most experiments of the ergodic kind. Compare Brian McHale (1992, 183–85). See for instance James Meehan (1976), Warren Motte (1986), J. David Bolter and Michael Joyce (1987), Brenda Kay Laurel (1991), Eduardo Kac (1995), Robert Kendall (1996), and John Cayley (1995b).

it was shuffled. To me, the book had exhausted all its possible readings in the very enunciation of its constructive idea. Some of its pages might have been intensely "beautiful," but given the purpose of the book, that would have been a mere accident. Its only validity as an artistic event lay in its construction, its conception as a book that would tell not one but all the stories that could be told, albeit according to the directions (admittedly few) of an author (1989, 170).

It would be all too easy (and perhaps also unfair) to dismiss Eco's antiformalist reaction out of hand as reactionary aesthetic prejudice. After all, the "book" in question seems to anticipate, even ask for, just this kind of acid anticriticism. And Eco's honest response has not been refuted by later literary history. Saporta's *Composition* remains an "apocryphal" experiment, a footnote in the history of postmodernist poetics, at best. But framed in a book on the aesthetics of "the open work," these remarks inevitably subvert the "openness" of Eco's aesthetic project. It is perhaps particularly ironic that, writing at the moment when some of the most resonant ergodic experiments and thematizations were starting to appear (Nabokov, Cortázar, Borges, Calvino, the OuLiPo), Eco decides to foreclose on the "work in movement" in favor of the poetics of "linear text expression" modernists such as Joyce. In his later nonfiction he appears to ignore the "movement" forms altogether, to the unfortunate effect that his theories of aesthetics, semiotics, and interpretation are much less relevant for ergodic literature (and cybernetic media in general) than they could have been.

Close to the time of Saporta's work, in 1960, the word *cyborg* was coined—not by some science fiction writer, as is commonly believed, but by Manfred Clynes, an Australian neurologist working in the field of space medicine (Clynes and Kline 1960). Clynes constructed the term from the words *cyb*ernetic *org*anism and used it to describe the new symbiotic entity that results from the alliance between humans and technology in a closed, artificial environment such as a space capsule. After being slowly assimilated by the science fiction culture, cyborg became the main textual nexus for the many themes of technological invasion of the human body, supplanting both the robot and the spaceship as the key cultural icon of humanity's posthuman future. The cultural potency of the cyborg figure is due not least to its many interstitial positions between us and the machines, between the alien and the familiar, between dependency and enhancement, terror and life support, creation and destruction, metal and flesh. As such it formulates a popular theme that dates back to the Daedalian and Promethean myths of classical literature: the ambivalence of material self-enhancement.

Recently, the biologist, feminist, and historian of science Donna Haraway, in her influential essay "A Cyborg Manifesto" (1991), appropriated the cyborg concept as a subversive, ironic model for breaking down suppressive categories such as gender, nature, culture, race, originality, progress, and so forth. In her own words, a "cyborg exists when two kinds of boundaries are simultaneously problematic: 1) that between animals (or other organisms) and humans, and 2) that between self-controlled, self-governing machines (automatons) and organisms, especially humans (models of autonomy). The cyborg is the figure born of the interface of automaton and autonomy" (1992, 139). Haraway invites us to the pleasures of blurring borders but, at the same time, recommends responsibility in our construction of new boundaries. To Haraway, the most significant metaphor for this border war is the relation between organism and machine, which, empowered by the new technologies, challenges the old Western dualisms of self/other, soul/body, male/female, whole/part, reality/appearance, and so on. The symbiosis between organism and machine must be admitted or accepted if a political platform of any epistemological endurance is to be constructed. Implied in this assault on totalization and organic integrity is a good-bye to Western humanism, inspired by Michel Foucault's claim that "man is an invention of recent date. And one perhaps nearing its end" (Foucault 1973, 387; see also Springer 1991, 322). Writing, suggests Haraway, "is pre-eminently the technology of cyborgs" (Haraway 1991, 176), and she sees the practice of textual self-construction and representation as the most potent weapon for political empowerment. That particular view is not pursued further here, but inspired by the notion of "cyborg literacy" I instead examine whether Haraway's perspective can help us explore the aesthetics of ergodic communication.

If we see the text as a kind of machine, a symbiosis of sign, operator and medium (cf. fig. 1.1), then the cyborg perspective is already
implied. This symbiosis is in no way pure and simple and can be
dissolved theoretically in a number of different ways, but all individual texts must somehow be positioned according to these three
fundamentals. If one is unaccounted for, there can be no text. For
instance, the strange "face" on the surface of Mars is a text only because (1) it has the shape of a face sign, (2) it has been identified as
such by someone, and (3) it is produced physically by optical and
geological conditions. Take away one of these, and *it* would not exist.
This is of course trivial, and I mention it only to draw attention
to the interplay between these categories, which is a cyborg relationship between organic and inorganic processes. "The text itself"
cannot be subsumed by either side of the triangle and remains at
the interstice, refusing to be reduced to either a linguistic, historic,
or material phenomenon, while depending on all three.

If this is so, differences between texts can be described in terms
of differences along these three dimensions. It might be tempting to
try to construct an entire ontology from this theoretical basis and
to formulate a three-dimensional matrix in which every text imaginable could be placed, but this seems both impossible and unneces-
sary. Impossible, because the three categories are infinite; unneces-
sary, because the diversity of existing textual phenomena are more
than sufficient to form the empirical basis for a relevant theory. So
instead of exploring these categories directly, which is impossible, I
assume that they cannot be examined independently, any more than
the category of "the text itself." We must therefore acknowledge the
theoretical character of these dimensions and use them to construct
the field of textual variation, which also is a field of cyborg aesthetics.

Any cyborg field, as any communicative field, is dominated by
the issue of domination or control. The key question in cyborg aesthetics is therefore, Who or what controls the text? Ideologically,
there are three positions in this struggle: author control, text control, and reader control. Author control comes closest to Barthes's
concept of the readable (*lisible*) text, where neither signifiers nor
interpretations are left to chance (Barthes 1975). Text control is

usually characterized as the programed play of elements and structures, so that the process of sign production is both unpredictable and original, with creative responsibility transferred to the machinery. Reader control puts the creative initiative on the users, who must assemble the available building blocks and make artistic sense according to their individual preferences. But how well do these ideological positions, and the importance of who is in control, correspond to aesthetic practice?

John Cayley's *Book Unbound* (1995a) is a literary work not easily classified by traditional aesthetics. As a computer program (written in Hypercard), it takes over the screen and spits forth short suggestive sentences one word at a time. Here is an example:

> it is not just the essential definitive icon
> the metaphor survives but its shape and significance change forever
> for the codex will live on it has not been static although its shape and
> significance change the book is the
> book is potentially a body of work a metaphor which may invoke any
> point has not been the book is not
> the book this dominance but the book the book is more difficult to
> believe that the InterNet
> the book is that it should be unwilling to apply a question of these
> fragments organized
> made sense of bound or bounded that the book is not the InterNet
> books libraries on the use of these machines
> the word is applied to bodies of text which the book the the the book is
> changing
> the sense of bound together for others this the words of bound
> together for others this longing is
> more difficult to believe that the the the codex will allow others this
> metaphor are elegant

The program assembles these lines from its hidden texts according to certain algorithms. As the process goes on, the hidden text is changed by what is displayed, and the user can select passages for inclusion in the regenerative process. Thus the text output is influenced and will be different for each copy of the text. Is it still the same text? Cayley calls the produced output "holograms," fragments that contain holographic versions of the initial material. The following sources are involved in the text production: (1) the initial hidden texts, which are not displayed directly but transmuted and interspersed with each other and the user-selected passages, (2) the mechanisms of the production, which are controlled by internal rules specified by the programer, and (3) the user's selection of fragments, based on personal preference.

This text is an impurity, a site of struggle between medium, sign, and operator. The fragments produced are clearly not authored by anyone. They are pulverized and reconnected echoes of meaning, and the meaning that can be made from them is not the meaning that once existed. *Book Unbound* is an extreme paragon of cyborg aesthetics, an illustration of the issue of communicative control. The pleasure of this text is far from accidental; it belongs not to the illusion of control but to the suggestive reality of unique and unrepeatable signification. It would be a grave mistake to see this text as a metaphor of the "impossibility of perfect communication" or as the embodiment of the gap between sign and meaning in texts. Instead, it shows how meaning struggles to produce itself through the cyborg activity of writing.

Three

Textonomy:
A Typology of Textual Communication

Ever since the poststructuralist and reader-oriented turns in literary theory, it has become increasingly clear that the linear communication model originally proposed by C. Shannon and W. Weaver (1969) and later appropriated and developed by Roman Jakobson (1960) is not representative of the complicated processes that go on between readers and texts. Both reader response and poststructuralism have responded to the structuralists' linear model with models that question the simple linear relationship among author, text, and reader; however, both approaches lack, to a greater or lesser extent, the formal clarity of their predecessor.

With the advent of computer media such as hypertext, the questions of reader and text have been both revitalized and crystallized, although it may be argued, contrary to the claims that hypertext is the embodiment of "the" poststructuralist concept of text (cf. Moulthrop 1989; Bolter 1991; Landow 1992a), that they are no longer the same questions. However, since the differences between the old and the new textual forms and reader positions are quite visible and tangible, relations between readers and the various types of texts are now relatively easy to describe categorically and formally. This chapter surveys these formal differences with the intent of setting up a typology to describe any textual medium. When a new textual type appears, as frequently happens these days, either the model must be able to describe it or it must be modified to be able to do so. As the new media have become visible, they also inspire us to look at the old media in a new light. It then becomes clear that the "stability of the printed book" is just as metaphysical and illusory as the present claims of a new electronic writing that alters the func-

A version of this chapter has been published as "Text, Hypertext, or Cybertext? A Typology of Textual Modes Using Correspondence Analysis," in *Research in Humanities Computing*, edited by Giorgio Perissinotto, Susan Hockey, and Nancy Ide (Oxford: Clarendon, 1996), 5:1–16.

tions of textual communication in singular and revolutionary ways (cf. Aarseth 1994).

As we saw in the discussion of the terms *nonlinear* and *multilinear*, a major problem in recent discussions of computer media is a lack of rigorous terminology. The discussion of these terms, while intrinsic to the question of hypertext, shows that the field of computer mediated textuality is in need of a terminology that has distinctive power as well as unproblematic connotations. Since the term *nonlinear* is somewhat broad and unclear, as well as negatory, I do not use it as an active term in this typology but as a corrective. Instead, a terminology is constructed that is not grounded in computer industrial rhetoric (cf. *hypertext, interactive, virtual,* etc.) but purely on observable differences in the behavior between text and reader (user).

For reasons of formality, not even the physical differences of the media (such as paper vs. phosphor screen) are given substantial status: as evidenced by the history of the media, the physical stratum of the medium does not necessarily influence the user-text relationship. An illustration of this is the transition from long-playing records to compact discs in the music industry, where the analog-to-digital shift of the artifact did not change any substantial aspects of the cultural production or consumption of music. I dwell on this point to support my approach of reconfiguring the terminology into a more functional and less ad hoc perspective. Since there are paper texts that function more like some digital texts than other texts in the same physical medium, the paper-digital dichotomy cannot be given analytical power as such, but it must be further examined if we wish to determine the exact significance of the materiality of the medium. The false simplicity of these terms must be abandoned, just as the poststructuralists deconstructed the simple dichotomies of the structuralists. In their place, a more discerning model based on empirical observations, able to accommodate future media patterns, must be constructed.

Previous Efforts

A few previous attempts have been made to typologize media diversity; of particular interest are Jan Bordewijk and Ben van

Kaam (1986) and Richard Ziegfeld (1989). Bordewijk and van Kaam present a typology of four modes of information "traffic patterns": *allocution, consultation, registration, and conversation,* which are ordered by two questions: Who owns the information? and Who controls the program for information access? Each of these questions are answered by "individual consumer" or "central provider" (19). These discursive modes seem to describe well the power relations between information providers and consumers, which is Bordewijk and van Kaam's main concern. In our context, however, where textual rather than social systems are being discussed, their model is less directly relevant.

Of greater relevance, but also more problematic, is Ziegfeld, who undertakes to compare the elements of "interactive fiction" with those of other media. Ziegfeld introduces a variety of "software options" (movement, simulation, interaction, etc.), which he relates to various literary elements (350), and while his effort was a valuable inspiration for my own present attempt, his categories appear underdefined and sometimes overlapping: Interaction "allows authors to enter into a dialogue with readers. Also, if the author chooses, interaction allows the reader to participate in the creation process" (347), while individualization is "letting the authors or readers control the text's shape" (356). Unfortunately, Ziegfeld's stimulating essay is marred by its own lack of conceptual rigor and focus of interest.

Finally, we should note Michael Joyce's distinction between exploratory and constructive hypertexts (1988)—texts that can be explored versus texts that can be changed, added to, and reorganized by the user—which has influenced my own categories of user functions.

Method

I categorize texts according to the typology. Then, using the program *Analytica* developed by Daniel Apollon (see Apollon 1990) at the University of Bergen, I employ correspondence analysis, a branch of exploratory data analysis developed mainly by the French data analysis school of Jean-Paul Benzecri (see Greenacre 1984). This method enables us to analyze categories and variables as well as objects, allowing us to link categories and objects. Variables that can describe substantial differences between the textual modes can then be singled out.

Although correspondence analysis has been applied to a wide variety of disciplines and problems, ranging from textual criticism to economics and archaeology, I am not aware of any previous applications in the field of literary genre or textual media typologies. I have previously used the method to describe media variety in computer games (Aarseth 1995), but it seems that very few literary applications exist (for an example, see McKinnon 1989). The technique was not developed with this kind of application in mind, and my approach seems fairly unrepresentative of mainstream applications of this method. So although the method itself is well established, in this context it should be considered tentative.

Of course, my approach is not without problems and limitations. Regarding the typology, it could be argued that the choice of variables is arbitrary and that quite different taxonomies would better achieve the same purpose. But even if this particular choice of variables and values ultimately were rejected, the general idea of such a multidimensional model deserves separate evaluation. Another potential problem pertains to the selection of samples. The texts are assembled eclectically, with the primary criterion that they be different from each other along at least one of the variables. Thus they are representative only of their own medium and not necessarily of any literary genre they might belong to. Many of them are unique in both respects, and the result of the analysis would be somewhat different if any of them were not included. There might also exist texts that I have overlooked in my search for diversity and that might have influenced the analysis substantially. Further, this search for diversity, along with the relatively small number of samples and the small number of possible values for each variable, produces data with much greater variation than a larger data set would have. We can therefore expect a less clustered distribution than is common and, therefore, a less obvious image to interpret and partition into synthetic genres. Also, the correspondence analysis, in order to synthesize the information down to two or three dimensions, must throw away a substantial percentage of that information.

The Typology

Before we can discuss differences between types of textual media, we must establish a common terminology and the basic concepts that apply to the objects under consideration. Since the focus of this analysis is textuality, we must be able to show that there is something textual about all the samples. So, what is a text? Or, what circumstances allow us to describe a certain object as a text? This question is both helped and hindered by the fact that no universal definition of *text* exists. Disciplines both within and outside of literary theory attach different meanings to the word, but the situation calls for a very pragmatic and broad definition, one that will reveal, rather than obscure, any inherent flaw.

A text, then, is any object with the primary function to relay verbal information. Two observations follow from this definition: (1) a text cannot operate independently of some material medium, and this influences its behavior, and (2) a text is not equal to the information it transmits. *Information* is here understood as a string of signs, which may (but does not have to) make sense to a given observer. It is useful to distinguish between strings as they appear to readers and strings as they exist in the text, since these may not always be the same. For want of better terms, I call the former *scriptons* and the latter *textons.* Their names are not important, but the difference between them is. In a book such as Raymond Queneau's sonnet machine *Cent mille milliards de poèmes* (Queneau 1961), where the user folds lines in the book to "compose" sonnets, there are only 140 textons, but these combine into 100,000,000,000,000 possible scriptons. In addition to textons and scriptons, a text consists of what I call a traversal function—the mechanism by which scriptons are revealed or generated from textons and presented to the user of the text. Scriptons are not necessarily identical to what readers actually read, which is yet another entity (a *lexie* in the Barthesian sense?) and one not determined by the text. Instead, scriptons are what an "ideal reader" reads by strictly following the linear structure of the textual output.

The following variables allow us to describe any text according to their mode of traversal:

1. *Dynamics:* In a static text the scriptons are constant; in a dy-

namic text the contents of scriptons may change while the number of textons remains fixed (intratextonic dynamics, or IDT), or the number (and content) of textons may vary as well (textonic dynamics, or TDT). A hypertext such as *Afternoon* (Joyce 1990) will have a fixed number of scriptons (and textons), while the game *Adventure* (Crowther and Woods 1976) will have a fixed set of textons but a variable number of scriptons (texton combinations), determined by the progress of the play. In a MUD, where other concurrent users can type in anything, the number of textons is not known.

2. *Determinability:* This variable concerns the stability of the traversal function; a text is determinate if the adjacent scriptons of every scripton are always the same; if not, the text is indeterminate. In some adventure games, the same response to a given situation will always produce the same result. In other games, random functions (such as the use of dice) make the result unpredictable.

3. *Transiency:* If the mere passing of the user's time causes scriptons to appear, the text is transient; if not, it is intransient. Some texts (e.g., Gibson's *Agrippa;* see Gibson 1992) scroll by their users at their own pace, while others do nothing unless activated by the user.

4. *Perspective:* If the text requires the user to play a strategic role as a character in the world described by the text, then the text's perspective is personal; if not, then it is impersonal. A text such as Italo Calvino's *If on a Winter's Night a Traveler . . .* (Calvino 1993) pretends to involve the reader as a participant, but there is nothing for the real reader to do but read. In a MUD, on the other hand, the reader is (in part) personally responsible for what happens to his or her character.

5. *Access:* If all scriptons of the text are readily available to the user at all times, then the text is random access (typically the codex); if not, then access is controlled. In a codex novel, you may turn to any passage at any time, directly from any other point. In a hypertext such as *Victory Garden,* to get to a specific passage you must typically follow an arbitrary path involving other specific passages before you get what you want. In other words, hypertexts without free text search capabilities are more, not less, linear than the codex.

6. *Linking:* A text may be organized by explicit links for the user

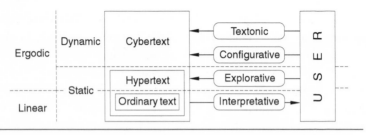

Figure 3.1. User Functions and Their Relation to Other Concepts

to follow, conditional links that can only be followed if certain conditions are met, or by none of these (no links). In *Afternoon,* some scriptons can be reached only after the reader has visited certain other scriptons. This makes *Afternoon* different from other hypertexts, where usually all links from a scripton are simultaneously available. Other texts, such as story generators, do not rely on links at all.

7. *User functions:* Besides the interpretative function of the user, which is present in all texts, the use of some texts may be described in terms of additional functions: the explorative function, in which the user must decide which path to take, and the configurative function, in which scriptons are in part chosen or created by the user. If textons or traversal functions can be (permanently) added to the text, the user function is textonic. If all the decisions a reader makes about a text concern its meaning, then there is only one user function involved, here called interpretation. In a forking text, such as Cortázar's *Rayuela* (Cortázar 1966), the reader must also explore, by making strategic choices about alternative paths and, in the case of adventure games, alternative actions. Some texts allow the user to configure their scriptons by rearranging textons or changing variables. And finally, in some cases the users can extend or change the text by adding their own writing or programing.

Together, these seven variables create a multidimensional space of 576 unique media positions ($576 = 3 \times 2 \times 2 \times 2 \times 2 \times 3 \times 4$). A text classified by this typological model will have a profile (e.g., static, determinate, transient, impersonal, controlled, none, configurative), which identifies it as belonging to a specific class of the 576 genre positions. In the correspondence analysis, this multi-dimensional space will be reduced to two synthetic axes, with a two-dimensional position for each of the texts and categories. If the model should be shown to contain errors (such as misreadings, inconsistencies, or idiosyncrasies) that render it unacceptable, a better model can be constructed and displayed following the same principles.

To sum up the typology, we have the following variables and values:

Variable	Possible value
Dynamics	Static, IDT, TDT
Determinability	Determinable, indeterminable
Transiency	Transient, intransient
Perspective	Permanent, impermanent
Access	Random, controlled
Linking	Explicit, conditional, none
User function	Explorative, configurative, interpretative, textonic

The four user functions and their relation to other concepts are shown in figure 3.1. The arrows symbolize the flow of information. Comparing these functions to our notions of static and dynamic text, we may define an ergodic text as one in which at least one of the four user functions, in addition to the obligatory interpretative function, is present. Not incidentally, this figure might also be seen as a depiction of a cybernetic feedback loop between the text and the user, with information flowing from text to user (through the interpretative function) and back again (through one or more of the other functions).

The Texts

A diverse set of texts, ranging from ancient China to the Internet, are the materials I analyze. The approach is qualitative, and the selection is based on the texts' distinctive user relationships, rather than on any popularity, literary quality, or seminal position they might enjoy. The oldest of these texts is the *I Ching* (ca. 1000 B.C.), the Chinese book of oracular wisdom that is used (rather than simply read) in a ritual that involves writing down a question, manipulating coins or yarrow stalks to produce a path (out of 4,096 possible paths) through the text, and consulting certain of the book's sixty-four fragments to reach an answer to the question.

Other texts include Apollinaire's *Calligrammes* (1916; see Apollinaire 1966), poems that fork out on the page; Raymond Queneau's *Cent mille milliards de poèmes* (1961); and *The Money Spider* by Robin Waterfield and Wilfred Davies (1988), a typical gamebook in which the reader must solve a puzzle by choosing the right path through the many fragments of the text. Another gamebook, *Falcon 5: The Dying Sun*, by Mark Smith and Jamie Thomson (1986), adds indeterminacy by having the player roll dice to decide between paths. *Pale Fire*, Vladimir Nabokov's 1962 novel, lets the reader skip between a long poem and its annotations, in which the main plot resides. Marc Saporta's novel, *Composition No. 1* (1962), consists of loose sheets that the reader shuffles and reads in a random sequence. Julio Cortázar's novel, *Hopscotch* (1966), can be read with alternate paths through the chapters. And the artist's book *Norisbo*, by Norwegian artist Randi Strand (1992a), folds from all four sides, so the reader reads a unique sequence folded by the last reader and then folds the pages to leave a unique combination for the next reader. All of these texts are paper based rather than computerized, yet they behave in ways that many theorists would reserve for electronic texts.

A number of digital texts are also included: the original *Adventure* game by William Crowther and Don Woods (1976); another, more flexible adventure game, *Twin Kingdom Valley*, by Trevor Hall (1983); the hypertext novels *Afternoon*, by Michael Joyce (1990), and *Victory Garden*, by Stuart Moulthrop (1991c); the conversation programs Eliza, by Joseph Weizenbaum (1966), and the unpredictable Racter, by Thomas Etter and William Chamberlain (1984); the prose generator by James Meehan, Tale-spin, and the network-based, multiuser adventure game *MUD1*, programed by Richard Bartle and Roy Trubshaw (1980). A later system, *TinyMUD*, designed by James Aspnes (1989), is user programable and was played and co-written by a number of people between August 1989 and April 1990. A standard narrative work, Herman Melville's *Moby Dick* (1851), represents the canonized mode of textuality.

Jenny Holzer's installation, *I Am Awake at the Place Where Women Die* (1993), is a linear electronic text projected by an LED sign, which endlessly repeats its short, painful messages. William Gibson's encrypted poem *Agrippa* (1992) is similarly displayed moving over a computer screen, but it can be read only once in unencrypted form. Allen S. Firstenberg's *The Unending Addventure* (1995) is a forking text on the World Wide Web that users can add notes to at the ends of the branches. Finally, there is John Cayley's *Book Unbound* (1995a), a holographic sentence generator that merges and mutates other texts, inviting readers to feed their favorite results back into the system. The twenty-three texts, classified according to the variables of our typology, are shown in table 3.1.

Analysis and Results

A multiple correspondence analysis performed on the above data matrix, using *Analytica*, gives the values shown in table 3.2. By this method, the seven dimensions of our data can be condensed to fewer dimensions or axes (1–4) of synthetic variables, with the first two axes accounting for 49 percent of the variance in the data set. With three axes, we get 64 percent. These axes are the ones used in the visualization, as each of the others add relatively little to the accuracy. The third axis, it turns out, is not very interesting: it shows mainly that the text *Agrippa* is very different from all the others; that is, it has an unusual combination of attributes that positions it far way from the other texts in the three-dimensional space of the three main axes. With this in mind, we can concentrate our interpretation on axes one and two.

When describing the data by only the two first dimensions, we give up 51 percent of the completeness, but that is the price we pay for readability. As pointed out by Michael J. Greenacre (1984, 7): "This is a general principle that permeates all descriptive statistical methods, namely that there is a trade-off between ease of interpretation and completeness of description. . . . The usefulness of a technique like correspondence analysis is that the gain in inter-

Table 3.1. Texts, by Typology Variables

Texts	Dynamics	Determinability	Transiency	Perspective	Access	Linking	User functions
Adventure	IDT	Determinable	Intransient	Permanent	Controlled	Conditional	EF
Afternoon	Static	Determinable	Intransient	Impermanent	Controlled	Conditional	EF
Agrippa	IDT	Determinable	Transient	Impermanent	Controlled	Explicit	IF
Book Unbound	TDT	Indeterminable	Transient	Impermanent	Controlled	Conditional	TF
Calligrammes	Static	Determinable	Intransient	Impermanent	Random	None	EF
Cent Mille Milliards	Static	Determinable	Intransient	Impermanent	Random	None	CF
Composition No. 1	Static	Indeterminable	Intransient	Impermanent	Controlled	None	IF
Eliza	IDT	Determinable	Intransient	Permanent	Controlled	Conditional	CF
Falcon	IDT	Indeterminable	Intransient	Permanent	Controlled	Conditional	EF
Holzer	Static	Determinable	Transient	Impermanent	Controlled	None	IF

Hopscotch	Static	Determinable	Intransient	Impermanent	Random	Explicit	EF
I Ching	Static	Indeterminable	Intransient	Permanent	Controlled	Conditional	CF
Moby Dick	Static	Determinable	Intransient	Impermanent	Random	None	IF
Money Spider	IDT	Determinable	Intransient	Permanent	Controlled	Conditional	EF
MUD1	TDT	Indeterminable	Transient	Permanent	Controlled	Conditional	EF
Norisbo	Static	Indeterminable	Intransient	Impermanent	Controlled	None	CF
Pale Fire	Static	Determinable	Intransient	Impermanent	Random	Explicit	IF
Racter	TDT	Indeterminable	Intransient	Permanent	Controlled	Conditional	CF
Tale-spin	TDT	Indeterminable	Intransient	Impermanent	Controlled	None	CF
TinyMUD	TDT	Indeterminable	Transient	Permanent	Controlled	Conditional	TF
Twin Kingdom Valley	TDT	Indeterminable	Intransient	Permanent	Controlled	Conditional	EF
Unending Addventure	Static	Determinable	Intransient	Permanent	Controlled	Explicit	TF
Victory Garden	Static	Determinable	Intransient	Impermanent	Controlled	Explicit	EF

Table 3.2. Correspondence-Analysis Result

Number	Eigenvalue	Inertia	Cumulated
1	0.48917210	31.13	31.13
2	0.28675256	18.25	49.38
3	0.22897193	14.57	63.95
4	0.15152210	9.64	73.59

pretability far exceeds the loss in information." The texts, as shown in figure 3.2, are distributed fairly evenly among the four quadrants. The outer limit seems to resemble a rough triangle, with *Adventure/Money Spider*, *TinyMUD*, and *Moby Dick* as the corners. (Since *Adventure*'s and *Money Spider*'s values are identical, they occupy the same position.) If we compare each quadrant of the plot with conventional genre partitions, we see that the northwest quadrant is dominated by typical adventure games (all but Eliza) and that the northeast quadrant is similarly (but not so strongly) occupied by forking texts and hypertexts. The southeast quadrant is less homogeneous, and in the southwest we find the most unpredictable and user-oriented group of samples.

Before we look at the positions of the categories, let us briefly consider the dichotomy, made by Bolter and others, between printed books and electronic texts (see Bolter 1991, 7). Ten of the samples are paper texts. When we look at their distribution (figure 3.3), we find that the two groups, instead of clustering together and away from each other, are largely overlapping. In light of our typology, then, there is no evidence that the electronic and printed texts have clearly divergent attributes. The range of variation within each group is much larger than the variation between the groups. However, two of the corners on the triangle are clearly dominated by each of the groups, so a closer look at the determining categories may give us some idea of what values are most typically associated with each group. In figure 3.4 textonic user configuration, textonic dynamics, and transient temporality characterize the electronic texts, while random access and static scriptons dominate the paper-inhabited area. However, it would not be correct to conclude

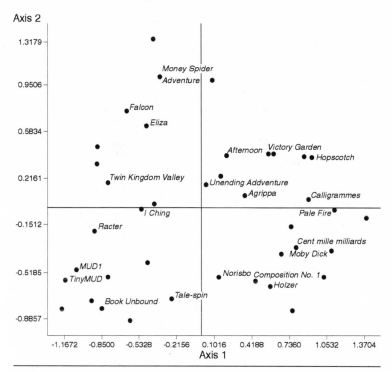

Figure 3.2. The Texts (unmarked dots are the categories; see figure 3.4)

that these values define a general distinction between paper texts and electronic texts, and as we can see, the versatility and divergence of paper texts are almost as great as that of digital texts. The distance between any two categories in figure 3.4 indicates how likely it is that both will describe a given text. Thus personal perspective and conditional linking are often, but not always, found together. No linking and the explorative user function, on the other hand, are an unlikely combination, but it is still found in *Calligrammes*. This tells us that any genre constructed from this two-dimensional map is pragmatic and not absolute. The text positions near the axes (*Calligrammes* is a typical example) are usually attracted by categories from different quadrants.

Since each of the positions in this model is a well-defined class

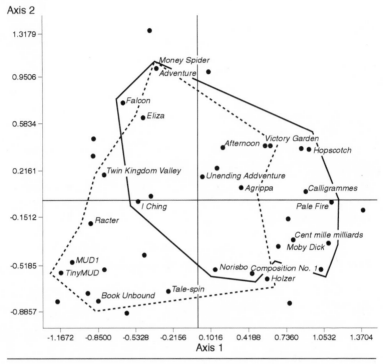

Figure 3.3. Electronic Text (dotted line) and Paper Text (solid line)

by itself, we do not have to construct larger, generalized genre categories, but it is of course tempting to do so, not least to see how well they correspond with conventional notions. There seem to be at least three different ways to partition the material. The first and simplest is to follow the primary axis and divide the plot into two areas, west and east. In the west we find most of the ludic texts, those that invite the user to role-play and to creatively participate. In the east we find calmer, more contemplative texts, with fewer features but also freer access. If we divide the plot according to the second axis, we find a clear group in the north, identical to the adventure game corner of the triangle and dominated by intratextonic dynamics and the exploring user function; in the south there is a clear split between east and west. This brings us back to the tri-

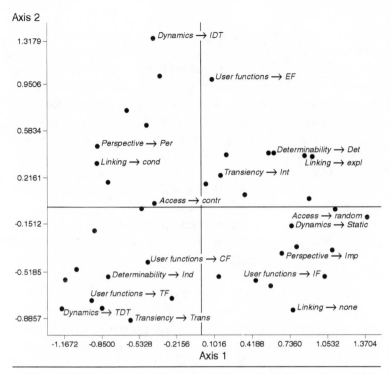

Figure 3.4. The Categories (unmarked dots are the texts; see figure 3.2)

angle model, which provides three poles: static texts (southeast), adventure games (north), and unpredictable texts (MUDs and text generators, southwest). North is further divided between adventure games (northwest) and hypertexts (northeast). The southeast is best described by interpretive user function and no linking. Further subdivisions may be useful, such as between the MUDs and text generators in the southwest, but I leave this to the reader's imagination.

Conclusions

The concept of text, always contested and problematized, is once again under reconfiguration. Should we use the same term for phenomena as diverse as *Moby Dick* and MUDs? Or for that matter, the *I Ching* and *Moby Dick*? If the answer is yes, we face some hard rethinking about the subject of media analysis. What are the common features of these different species? The main question here is user activity. Any text directs its user, by convention, mechanism, or social interaction. The reader is (and has always been) a necessary part of the text, but one that we now realize can (or must) perform more than one function. If these are all texts, perhaps the word *reader* no longer has any clear meaning. However, if the answer is no, we still have to construct a viable terminology to describe the literary games and rhetorical rituals we can observe both in the new media and in the old papery ones. There is still much to be said for the concept of text, and the various samples examined here in no way invalidate the category. The important lesson to be learned from discontinuous and forking texts is that when two readers approach a text they do not have to encounter the same words and sentences in order to agree that it probably was the same text. And this is not new: it is a classical feature of reading, as Roland Barthes points out in his comment on tmesis (1975).

The typological approach is one way to question conceptions about texts, readers, and the limits of such concepts. Its reductionist perspective makes it easy to check, criticize, modify, or even reject if necessary. The larger categories attained by this method explain themselves through their construction, and the problem of industrial-rhetorical terminology that haunts so much of the current theoretical discussions of the new media can thereby, we hope, be avoided. The same approach could probably be used in other typological studies of cultural phenomena, such as the study of literary genres. The open categories approach also allows for a prediction of hypothetical textual modes, by combining functions that are not found together in any existing texts. Thus the model works both on an abstract, synthesizing level and on a particularizing, predictive one. The paper-electronic dichotomy is not supported by our findings. It is revealing and refreshing to observe how flexible and dynamic a book printed on paper can be, and this gives us an important clue to the emergence of digital text forms: new media do not appear in opposition to the old but as emulators of features and functions that are already invented. It is the development and evolution of codex and print forms, not their lack of flexibility, that make digital texts possible.

But perhaps even more disputable than the issue of these textual genres' various capabilities, is the question of what to call them. There is a tendency among hypertext theorists to call all electronic texts *hypertexts* (and to call paper-based texts with paths or similar devices *protohypertexts*), but this sort of imperialist classification is not useful, considering the wide variety of textual types (many of which are already known by other names, such as MUDs and adventure games). *Hypertext* is a useful term when applied to the structures of links and nodes, but it is much less so if it includes all other digital texts as well. I suggest the term *cybertext* for texts that involve calculation in their production of scriptons. This criterion corresponds nicely to all the texts in the west half of figures 3.2, 3.3, and 3.4, while in the east it only applies to *Afternoon*, which is not really a pure hypertext, since some of its links are conditional. The concept of cybertext is therefore highly relevant to the interpretation of our analysis, since it almost perfectly follows the division established by the main axis. To distinguish further between the southwest and northwest quadrants, we might borrow Michael Joyce's terms and describe the southwest texts as constructive cybertexts and the northwest group as exploratory.

It might seem smug to suggest cybertext as a main category in the study of textual media variation and behavior, but at least it fits the current typological study quite well. This result actually came as a surprise to me. I had not planned for it, "calculation" not being one of my formal categories.

Four

No Sense of an Ending:
Hypertext Aesthetics

Live in fragments no longer. — E. M. Forster

The theoretical problems posed by the literary hypertext *Afternoon* (Joyce 1990) — such as the relationship between modernist poetics and hypertext technology — can be investigated using theories of rhetoric and narratology.

When considering the literary field of hypertext writing, we should not content ourselves with looking only at the texts themselves. It is a common strategy among theorists in the field to combine the literary hypertexts (or, skipping those, a direct invocation of hypertext itself) with well-known literary-critical theories by Barthes, Bakhtin, Deleuze-Guattari, Derrida, Foucault, Iser, Lacan, and others. While such approaches are useful for establishing the legitimacy of the field and have produced some very fine essays, they do not contribute to an understanding of the construction of the field itself — not surprisingly, since they are part of it. We might characterize these attempts as the quest for a poetics of hypertext, in contrast to the following, which is an attempt to analyze the aesthetics of hypertext, the possible motives that produce both the hypertexts and their poetics.

Hypertext is often understood as a medium of text, as an alternative to (among others) the codex format found in books, magazines, and bound manuscripts. It is often described as a mechanical (computerized) system of reading and writing, in which the text is organized into a network of fragments and the connections between them. As such, it has obvious potential benefits: A reader may approach a specific point of interest by a series of narrowing choices simply by clicking on the screen with the mouse. This allows for much more convenient use than the codex, where the transition between two nonadjoining places can be slow and distractive. However, for such a trait to be useful, the text in question must contain the need for such transition as an intrinsic figure. The success of translating codex texts into hypertexts hinges, it seems to me, on the existence of such prefigurations. With hypertext for general, practical purposes (encyclopedias, reference manuals, textbooks) this becomes a political issue, namely the relative value of unicursal versus multicursal organization. This issue has deeply cognitive and pedagogical aspects, which I will not go into here. However, when applied to the field of literature, the issue is freed from utilitarian demands and, instead, becomes subjected to the more autonomous perspective of aesthetic criticism.

Hypertext literature (hereafter called hyperfiction) does not have to answer to the problems of practicality faced by nonliterary hypertext; or rather, it is free to answer in a literary way, by foregrounding the issues of mimesis and narrative in the manner that is expected of a literary work of art. Hyperfiction such as Michael Joyce's *Afternoon*, as we shall see, can be configured neatly into the literary canon of modernism by playing on the very figures that in nonliterary hypertext appear as the main unresolved problems of textual structure. (This is often referred to as the problem of navigation; cf. Bernstein 1991.)

When Ted Nelson first coined the word *hypertext* in 1965, he was thinking of a new way of organizing text so that it could be read in a sequence chosen by the reader, rather than followed only in the sequence laid down by the writer. However, since codex texts can also be read in sequences determined by the reader, what he in fact suggested was a system in which the writer could specify which sequences of reading would be available to the reader. Later, implementations of such systems, for example, *Storyspace*, embodied this suggestion so fully that readers could follow *only* the sequences laid down by the writer. Hyperfictions written in *Storyspace*, like *Afternoon*, do not allow its readers free browsing, unlike any codex fiction in existence. The reader's freedom from linear sequence, which is often held up as the political and cognitive strength of hypertext, is a promise easily retracted and wholly dependent on the hypertext system in question.

The activity of hypertext reading is often portrayed, in contrast to codex reading, as a kind of co-authorship, with the reader creating her own text as she goes along. This idea has done much to promote the myth of hypertext as a better "tool for the mind" than the older writing technologies. I doubt, however, that the effect of hypertext (in its many different implementations) can be singularly identified as a means to make reading and writing come together in a single process. The cognitive aspects of hypertext cannot be elaborated here, but in terms of literary theory, it is fair to say that the hypertexts we can observe today, from the novels published by Eastgate Systems to those freely available on the World Wide Web, operate well within the standard paradigm of authors, readers, and texts. Of course there are interesting side effects and novel possibilities resulting from the migration from one medium to another, but hypertext, especially when compared to other new digital media, is not all that different from the old world of print, pen, and paper. Hypertext is certainly a new way of writing (with active links), but is it truly a new way of reading? And is all that jumping around the same as creating a new text?

We might also ask if the discontinuous, fragmentary reading demanded by hypertext is not a form of tmesis (see Barthes 1975). But to assume this would be to make a grave mistake. Nevertheless, since it is a common trope among hypertext theorists to claim that hypertext "embodies" or "makes manifest" this or that literary or theoretical concept (a co-optive rhetoric that we might call the reificational fallacy), we must expect that tmesis may also be misappropriated in this manner. For Roland Barthes, tmesis is the reader's unconstrained skipping and skimming of passages, a fragmentation of the linear text expression that is totally beyond the author's control. Hypertext reading is in fact quite the opposite: as the reader explores the labyrinth, she can not afford to tread lightly through the text but must scrutinize the links and venues in order to avoid meeting the same text fragments over and over again (this is typical of *Afternoon*). Only a linear text sequence (with intransient temporality) can be read in a free tmesic manner, as the reader is free to skip passages defined entirely by him. Contradistinctively, tmesis in hypertext will always be limited by the topological constraints laid down by the author. We might say that hypertext punishes tmesis by controlling the text's fragmentation and pathways and by forcing the reader to pay attention to the strategic links. The disoriented movements of a reader looking for fresh links in a hypertext labyrinth (what I later call an ergodic aporia) might be confused with tmesis. This is not, however, Barthes's "textual bliss" but, rather, the reader's textual claustrophobia as he skims the *déjà-lu* nodes.

What ways of reading does hypertext invite? This depends on the hypertext system in question and its contents. But if codex text allows two basic ways—homolinear reading (with the line) and heterolinear reading (tmesis)—the hypertext structure of nodes and links only allows one: hyperlinear reading, the improvised selection of paths across a network structure. Of course, to mitigate the inflexibility caused by author-imposed fragmentation, most non-fiction hypertext systems include additional reader-oriented tools, such as free text search functions, multiple windows, and path-history lists. I argue elsewhere argue that, with the current differences between hypertext systems, not least those used for poetic purposes, it is dangerous to construct general theories about hyperliterature (Aarseth 1994, 67–69). Instead, we must look at each system as a potentially different technical medium, with aesthetically distinct consequences. Hypertext is as much an ideological category as a technological one, constructed by its presumed difference from, and superiority to, paper media, and we should take care not to let this myth subconsciously influence our readings of individual texts.

One example that illustrates this point is Stuart Moulthrop's hyperfiction *Hegirascope* (1995), published on the World Wide Web. The Web is an Internet-based hypertext system developed by Tim Berners-Lee and other researchers at CERN; it has, and has gained, immense popularity since its beginnings in the early nineties. It comes close to fulfilling Ted Nelson's (1987) dream of the "Docuverse," a global information system in which all the texts in the world are available to almost instant access and on which users may publish their own material and link their documents to any other document. The World Wide Web is based on the document description language HTML (hypertext markup language), but the most popular browser program for the Web, Netscape Navigator, uses a modified version of HTML that extends the interface with certain functions. One of these special functions, "client pulling," is exploited by Moulthrop in *Hegirascope* and makes the reading experience very different from what we are used to with other texts, hyper or not. In *Hegirascope*, the text fragments are "pulled," like a non-interruptible slide show, after a specified number of seconds, typically fifteen to twenty, and replaced with the next fragment. This puts the reader under severe strain, forcing him to skim the text before it disappears, an ironic subversion of the traditional modus operandi of the Web surfer. In addition, *Hegirascope's* text nodes contains normal links, which give the reader some slight sense of control, but he is left with the feeling of rowing against the current in a mighty river.

In linear dynamic text formats, such as Jenny Holzer's electronic word streams, the reader is not required to act and can, therefore, relax in his role as observer (Holzer 1993). In *Hegirascope*, on the other hand, the reader is forced to reflect on the project of reading, the use or futility of it, in the most dramatic way yet invented. J. David Bolter makes a similar comment about *Afternoon:* "'Afternoon' is about the problem of its own reading" (1991, 127). *Hegirascope* can certainly be seen as a logical continuation of the epistemological experiment begun by *Afternoon*. But where *Afternoon*, according to Bolter, poses a geometrical problem, in which the reader "must gain an intuition of the spatial structure" (127), *Hegirascope* adds a temporal figure, which can be seen as an allegory of the reader's lack of influence over the text and, on a more general scale, of the partial in any process of reading: texts do not "sink in," they just stimulate the reader's eternal process of meaning.

"This is not a novel," Moulthrop warns in the introductory note to *Hegirascope*, perhaps to dissuade repetitions of a critique against his and others' previous literary hypertexts that, for all their claims of novelty, were really novels in the well-established tradition of experimental fiction. And judging by both *Hegirascope's* temporal mode and its verbal content, here *novel* (in the literary sense) does not seem to fit as a description. The previous hypernovels could be contemplated at the reader's pace, just as any other novel, but *Hegirascope* does not allow for contemplative reading, which is perhaps the most important feature of the genre. *Hegirascope* has left the stationary, reader-relative, space-time position of previous literature and gone where no literature has gone before—except, perhaps, for adventure games and MUDs, but this is not really a fair comparison. The added effect of the temporal pull turns *Hegirascope* into a hypertext parody, an excessive fragmentation that overheats the medium, as Marshall McLuhan (who is, perhaps not incidentally, one of the characters) might have said (see McLuhan 1964).

Less dramatic, but just as significant, is the ontological difference between World Wide Web documents like *Hegirascope* and the modern text media that precede them. Before the Internet, literary mass publication irrevocably meant mass production, whether on paper, CD-ROM, or diskettes. With codex and hypertext alike, to get the word out one has to copy it so that identical physical objects can be sent over a large area. A World Wide Web document, on the other hand, exist fully only in one place—on the World Wide Web server where the author (or document owner) has placed it. The work of art thus regains a sense of place. And whereas a book or CD-ROM is beyond the author's control once it is sold, *Hegirascope's* author retains full control over its content even after the text is published. He may at any point change or add parts to the text, without any reader's knowledge, and he is the only one who has full comprehension of the text's composition at any time. The ontology of the Web text is close to that of a painting, where the artist may modify and revise the same work in a process that may take many years. With novels, revision after publication is not common, and happens, when it does, only once in most cases. But the Web text may be modified many times a day, with little effort.

It can be argued that this takes us into an new era in the history of art, one which we might call (pace Walter Benjamin) the "Age of Post-Reproduction" (see Benjamin 1992). Here, the work of art regains parts of its aura, its "here and now," through the sense that it cannot be fully copied and reproduced, since it has a singular place on the network and also a temporal dimension, a dynamic lifetime. As Roman Ingarden (1973) claims, the literary (and the musical) work of art has no temporal extension, since it may be performed in a different tempo each time. But a work that may be observed in different stages of completeness and that has not yet crystallized in a final version is both temporal and irreproducible. This new contemporaneity between artwork and observer found on nonlocal networks such as the Internet becomes a possible source of an aesthetics quite different from those of the traditional cultural industry of the mass media. Technologizing and digitalization do not by necessity lead to the posthuman existence of the simulacra that certain television-scared "critics" have blindly attributed to all modern technology.

Paradigms of Hypertext

The purpose of computers is human freedom, and so the purpose of hypertext is overview and understanding; and this, by the way, is why I disapprove of any hypertext (like Michael Joyce's *Afternoon*) that does not show you the interconnective structure. —Theodor Holm Nelson

This statement by Theodor Nelson is a good illustration of how readily the old conflict between the ideals of the Enlightenment and the poetics of modernism have migrated to the field of hypertext. This is hardly surprising, considering the fact that hypertext is a logical extension—and hardly a revolutionary substitution—of the communication technology that both the Enlightenment and modernist literature is based on. Contrary to Nelson's idealistic claim, the purpose of computers is power, and hypertext is as much involved in that struggle for power as anything else. Some might reject a text like Michael Joyce's *Afternoon* as a matter of taste, but when it is rejected as a matter of principle, the suspicion arises that *Afternoon* is telling us something that we do not like to hear and that, therefore, might be well worth listening to.

Recent studies of hypertext fiction, which more often than not use *Afternoon* as their prime example, are often concerned with showing how hypertext embodies the iconoclastic musings of the so-called poststructuralist movement. As J. David Bolter proclaims:

postmodern theorists from reader response critics to deconstructionists have been talking about text in terms that are strikingly appropriate to hypertext in the computer. When Wolfgang Iser and Stanley Fish argue that the reader constitutes the text in the act of reading, they are describing hypertext. When the deconstructionists emphasize that a text is unlimited, that it expands to include its own interpretations—they are describing a hypertext, which grows with the addition of new links and elements. When Roland Barthes draws his famous distinction between the work and the text, he is giving a perfect characterization of the difference between writing in a printed book and writing by computer (1992, 24).

What Bolter sees as hypertext's "vindication of postmodern literary theory" (24; but surely Iser is no postmodernist) is clearly a misalignment of the reader response (phenomenological) and the poststructuralist (semiological) concepts of text with the philological (material) concept of hypertext. To claim that hypertext is fulfilling "postmodern theory"—and that "postmodern theorists have been doing this [i.e., describing hypertext] without knowing it" (24)—is an attempt to colonize several rather different critical fields by replacing their empirical object or objects on the imperialist pretext that they did not really have one until now. Since the claim is based on a confusion of two different levels—between Ingarden's "real object" and "aesthetic object," that is, between physical reality and the construction in the observer's mind (see Chatman 1978, 26), and what a Hjelmslevian semiotician would see as the difference between the form of the expression and the form of the content (cf. Eco 1976, 51–52; Andersen 1990, 69–72)—it seems hardly necessary to refute it. However, since it also represents a dominant paradigm within the field of hypertext theory, I add a few comments (see also Moulthrop 1989; Bolter 1991; Landow 1992a).

Poststructuralism is a theoretical tradition that originated in a group of mostly French-writing critics and philosophers (Jacques Derrida, Roland Barthes, Julia Kristeva, Michel Foucault, and others) who, since the late sixties, have tried to show the inner contradictions of concepts such as *sign, structure, work,* and *author* in order to foreground the metaphysical nature of these innocent-looking terms. To demonstrate their points about the unstable relation between word and meaning, the illusion of originality, the social construction of authorship, and the intertextual relations of texts, some of these writers used words such as *network* and *link* to illustrate that texts are not isolated islands of meaning but ongoing dialogues of repetition, mutation, and recombination of signs. However, to read these theorists' claims as a call for a new type of text (hypertext) is to mistake their descriptive, epistemological investigation of signification (and their critique of certain previous paradigms) for a normative attack on the limits of a specific communication technology (printing). This portrayal of deconstruction as hypertext prophecy is doubly ironic, since it relies on the linking (in a hypertext fashion) of common (and often poorly translated) words from both sides (e.g., "network," "readerly") to demonstrate a common intention. As any deconstructor would tell us, identical signifiers do not guarantee identical meanings.

What hypertext and poststructuralism might have in common is a much more general aspect of textuality and writing: the need to refer to, repeat, and represent other texts; but this aspect is much older and more well established than both hypertext technology and deconstructive theory. Even though the study of hypertext fiction by means of poststructuralism has yielded many valuable insights, a lot of simpler, pressing questions have gone unanswered. For instance, in what sense can a hypertext be a narrative? Is hypertext a literary genre or a literary technique? How different is hypertext fiction from other types of fiction? Exactly what is implied in the claim made by George Landow (1992a, 117) that in hypertext "the reader is a reader-author"? In an interesting chapter called "Reconfiguring Narrative," Landow suggests that hypertext "calls into question ideas of plot and story current since Aristotle. Looking at the *Poetics* in the context of hypertext suggests one of two things: either one simply cannot write hypertext fiction (and the *Poetics* show why that would be the case) or else Aristotelian definitions and descriptions of plot do not apply to stories read and written within a hypertext environment" (101).

Landow's argument seems to rest on an unwritten assumption: that fiction and narrative are the same. This is indeed a common notion, but it is still not self-evident. Usually one distinguishes between fictional and factual (documentary) narrative, which would seem to make fiction a subcategory of narrative, but let me here suggest that narrative and fiction should be viewed as different *types* of categories and, therefore, independent of each other. Fiction, it seems to me, should be regarded as a category not of form but of content (i.e., the same sentence might be fact or fiction, depending on its reference). Narrative, on the other hand, is a formal category, even if its definitions may vary. Hypertext can therefore well be fiction without being narrative; it can simply be fiction in an different form. (It can also contain narration without being narrative, just like certain other literary genres.)

Let me suggest a third alternative to Landow's two: that hypertext fiction calls into question only the idea of hypertext story and plot, not story and plot as such.[1] Bolter, commenting on Joyce's *Afternoon*, is on the right track: "We could say that there is no story at all; there are only readings" (1991, 124). Thus hypertext is not a reconfiguration of narrative but offers an alternative to it, as I try to demonstrate through the concept of ergodics.

In the rest of this chapter, I examine some narratological problems posed by Michael Joyce's *Afternoon: A Story* (1990). I invoke a set of concepts that might help us describe hypertext narration in a more precise manner than is possible using standard literary terms, and I use these concepts in an attempt to understand what goes on in hypertext fiction. I realize that *Afternoon* is unrepresentative of the growing body of literary hypertexts, especially because of its invisible links (or "words that yield," in Joyce's terminology; cf. Harpold 1994, 214, n. 6) and because of the conditional access to parts of the text (although this latter feature seems to enjoy frequent use by what we might call the Storyspace school of hypertext). My conclusions are therefore not necessarily valid for other hypertexts, especially not for hypertext poems, although I hope these conclusions retain some generality that students of these other texts find useful. Hypertext poetry of course comes with its own set of theoretical challenges, which regrettably cannot here be given the space they deserve. A central problem lies in the term itself. Is a hypertext poem a poem? Or is it something else? It may be argued that clickable words and menus subvert the lyrical genre aspect by inviting the user to play an (imagined) personal role in the production of a

---

1. Aristotelian ideas of story and plot have been contested since Horace, as Wallace Martin (1986, 84) points out, so hypertext is in any case not a radically unprecedented critique of Aristotelian concepts.

reading path. The "poeticness" of a poem would thus be challenged by the readers' awareness of their own subjective actions. This may not be a bad idea at all, but it makes the text something other than the poems of the past (even Apollinaire's): perhaps a "hyperpoem," if we could only understand the difference.

But for now let us consider *Afternoon* as a piece of modernist writing.

The Sense of a Novel: Michael Joyce's *Afternoon*

In *The Sense of an Ending*, Frank Kermode characterizes Alain Robbe-Grillet's novel *Les Gommes* as "a novel in which the reader will find none of the gratification to be had from sham temporality, sham causality, falsely certain description, clear story. The new novel 'repeats itself, bisects itself, modifies itself, contradicts itself, without even accumulating enough bulk to constitute a past—and thus a "story," in the traditional sense of the word.' The reader is not offered easy satisfactions, but a challenge to creative co-operation" (1967, 19). Without doubt, this could easily be taken for an accurate description of *Afternoon*. But what it refers to is a French modernist novel from 1953, a work of codex-based literature, not hypertext. There are also other similarities: the quotation within the quotation is from Robbe-Grillet himself, who (like Joyce) has written extensively on his own poetics. Finally, both texts use the semi-Oedipean motive of a man investigating his own crime. This is not to suggest that the two texts are alike but rather that they seem to define very similar literary positions, like different questions for the same answer. Despite their obvious material differences, they seem to address the same narrative problems and evoke the same critical responses. Why?

Afternoon has often been labeled *postmodernist*, and it does contain many literary devices typically associated with postmodernism (the metonymic mixing of fragments and genres, self-commentary and intrusions by the "author," typographical variation, metaleptic breaks (for a spoof on interactive technologies and technologists, see figure 4.1). But in the hypertext environment of *Afternoon*, these devices are naturalized and therefore do not cause the subversion they might have in a codex format. So although *Afternoon* is play-

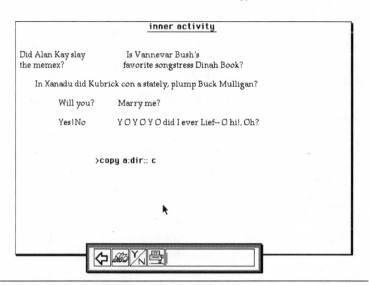

Figure 4.1. A Postmodernist Scripton in *Afternoon*

ing postmodernist games, these are marginalized by the modernist devices of jump, fragment, split perspectives, multiple threads, uncertain causalities, *ecriture labyrinthine*, and so on.[2] Or are they hypertext devices?

With a technologically immersed text like *Afternoon*, there is always the danger that its mechanical devices all but erase the poetical and narratological elements that are not directly effected through the technology. Instead of asking, What have I read? the critic might become preoccupied with the question, Have I read all? and come to identify the task of interpretation as a task of territorial exploration and technological mastery. But exploration cannot be the critic's primary task, and discussions about whether it takes fifty-seven or eighteen steps to get to a specific place in *Afternoon* is more like a game of trivia than a concern for criticism. In fact, *Afternoon* is not very hard to map, if one only believes that it can be done; it may take a day, given practice, patience, and a few sheets of plain

2. For another view on the relationship between modernism and postmodernism in hypertext, see Bjørn Sørenssen (1993).

paper: 539 places of text may sound like a lot, but take away the many one-word and one-letter fragments and what is left is about 300 smaller or larger pieces, roughly the equivalent of a hundred-odd codex pages. I stress these facts because *Afternoon* is often subjected to logistic hyperbole and mystification. Jane Yellowlees Douglas (1991, 117) compares *Afternoon* to the literally inexhaustible and infinite magic book in Jorge Luis Borges's 1962 short story "The Book of Sand" (Borges 1974). And Stuart Moulthrop (1989, 263) takes the word of the author at face value: "Joyce has said that 'Afternoon' has 'no flow chart' and that there is no sense in trying to map its complexities. The mysteries of the text's design and function are not meant to be penetrated." But more realistic and accurate descriptions of *Afternoon* do exist, notably J. David Bolter (1991, 123–27). As one of the programers behind *Storyspace*, *Afternoon's* hypertext system, Bolter is in an excellent position to demystify the text. *Afternoon* is certainly mapable; it can be loaded into the full version of *Storyspace* and its links studied there in detail.

The comparison between Robbe-Grillet and Joyce has been made before, notably by Douglas (1994) in her impressive close reading of *Afternoon*. She also argues convincingly that one does not need formal closure (or a singular "ending") to come away from the text satisfied. To describe the literary structure, she has proposed the terms *interactive narrative* and *stratigraphic writing*. However, my own experiences with *Afternoon* make me less appreciative of her proposed critical terminology than her excellent achievement as a decryptive critic. The term *interactive* is particularly problematic, as both Moulthrop (1989, 261) and Joyce (1991, 79) have pointed out. Even so, the ideological invocation of "interactive fiction" is appropriated repeatedly as a label for the literary hypertexts by their proponents, who see hyperfiction as the next step up from adventure games on the evolutionary ladder (cf. Bolter and Joyce 1987, Douglas 1991, Moulthrop 1994b). Others fear it may be too late for such an appropriation (cf. Harpold 1994, 215, n. 7). Ironically, one of the first, and unacclaimed, hyperfictions, Adam Engst's *Descent into the Maelstrom* (1989), emulated the second-person voice and perspective of the adventure game interface, thus demonstrating the kinship between the two media genres, much in the same way as the choose-your-own-adventure books had done previously.

The term *interactive fiction* implies an equality between the reader and author beyond that found in other literary texts. In my experience, the reader is as much at the constructor's mercy in *Afternoon* as in any difficult text, although in a different way. And although there certainly is narration (relation of events) in the text, that is not the same as a narrative. Interactive narrative might imply some sort of user-directed story generator, but *Afternoon* does not fit that description very well, as it relentlessly leads the reader in labyrinthine circles. By "stratigraphic," Douglas implies that *Afternoon* consists of (five) "layers" (1994, 172); but merely by using the standard reading version I have not been able to identify any hierarchical structure of this kind. A better term might be *heterarchic*, a structure of subverted hierarchies, or in the case of *Afternoon*, of well-connected nodes and remote threads, where ideas of "deepest" and "topmost" are meaningless. Typical of both modernism and *Afternoon* is the limited point of view (cf. McHale 1987, 14), in which the reader is denied access to any dominant hierarchic structure, and therefore caught in a heterarchy.

The idea of hypertext as heterarchy solves a problem in recent discussions about hypertextual poetics. Commenting on two conflicting views on hypertext-as-hierarchy, Moulthrop (1994c, 60) holds that "the answer . . . is both yes and no; hypertext abhors a hierarchy; hypertext is hierarchy." The concept of heterarchy engages the structural complexity of hypertext while avoiding Moulthrop's aporetic and paradoxical conclusion.

The connection between modernism and *Afternoon* is also confirmed by its author. In their 1987 article, "Hypertext and Creative Writing," Bolter and Joyce present hypertext as a "new kind of flexible, interactive fiction", "a continuation of the modern 'tradition' of experimental literature in print" (41). They see literary hypertext as belonging to the experimental tradition of "modernism, futurism, Dada surrealism, letterism, the nouveau roman, concrete poetry" by "disrupting the stability of the text" (44).

But is hypertext a modernist structure? No. If we take *Afternoon*

as proof of such a thesis, we are making two mistakes: We ignore the many nonhypertextual modernist elements in the text, and we take its hypertextual organization as typical of all hypertextual works. As I have pointed out, *Afternoon* relies heavily on classical modernist devices, from its "epistemological dominant" (i.e., the focus on conditions for knowledge; cf. McHale 1987) to its use of wordplay (e.g., "inner activity"). Also, the anchors and links in *Afternoon* are used in an idiosyncratic way and certainly not for the purpose of "overview and understanding" that Nelson (1992, 56) has in mind. If hypertext (like the codex) can be used to support the poetics of modernism (something *Afternoon* demonstrates successfully), it can be used equally well for quite adverse (cognitive or poetic) purposes (again, like the codex).

The Rhetoric of Hyperliterature: Aporia and Epiphany

Previous attempts to discuss hypertext rhetoric have mostly been concerned with what might just as accurately be called hypertext poetics: design rules for making communication by hypertext as efficient as possible (see Landow 1991; Slatin 1991; Moulthrop 1991d) or focused on the activity of hypertext production (Liestøl 1994). Here I wish to invoke rhetoric as a descriptive perspective on the aesthetic text; as a way of looking at "the text at work" by trying to discover some of its intrinsic tropes and figures rather than by looking at the construction of hypertextual objects from the constructor's point of view.

Drawing on the nineteenth-century rhetoric of Pierre Fontanier (1968), I have previously described the figure of "nonlinearity" as

> clearly not a trope, since it works on the level of words, not meaning; but it could be classified as a type of *figure*, following Pierre Fontanier's taxonomy of tropes and figures. In the second part of his classic inventory of rhetorical figures, *Figures du discours*, Fontanier defines "les figures non-tropes"—the figures other than tropes. These he divides into several classes: construction-figures, elocution-figures, style-figures, and thought-figures, with various subclasses including inversion, apposition, ellipsis, and repetition. Among these classes we could place the figures of nonlinearity, with the following set of subclasses: forking,

linking/jumping, permutation, computation, and polygenesis (Aarseth 1994, 80).

"Forking," as the simplest figure of nonlinearity, I located in graphically experimental texts such as Apollinaire's 1916 *Calligrammes* (Apollinaire 1966), in which the words and sentences on a page are spread out in many directions. "Linking/jumping" is clearly the hypertext master figure, while the others are associated with various forms of cybertext. This figure constitutes the "syntactical" level of hypertext rhetoric, as the device that orders and separates the semantic units of verbal information (link names, node headings, node text, etc.). But what, if any, are the tropes (semantic figures) of hypertext, especially the hypertext novel?

The main difference between *Afternoon* and other modernist texts is that *Afternoon* relies on the hypertext mechanism to alienate the reader, rather than for a linguistic effect. The engaged hypertext quickly turns into a dense, multicursal labyrinth, and the reader becomes not so much lost as caught, imprisoned by the repeating, circular paths and his own impotent choices. What we identify as fragments (what looks like fragments of a narrative), or rather the act of (false) identification itself, makes us look for a whole even if there is no evidence that the fragments ever constituted such a whole. This kind of impasse is a main trope of *Afternoon's* literary machine: an *aporia* in a very literal sense. In contrast to the aporias experienced in codex literature, where we are not able to make sense of a particular part even though we have access to the whole text, the hypertext aporia prevents us from making sense of the whole because we may not have access to a particular part. Aporia here becomes a trope, an absent pièce de résistance rather than the usual transcendental resistance of the (absent) meaning of a difficult passage.

Complementary to this trope stands another: the epiphany. This is the sudden revelation that replaces the aporia, a seeming detail with an unexpected, salvaging effect: the link out. The hypertext epiphany, unlike James Joyce's "sudden spiritual manifestation" (Abrams 1981, 54), is immanent: a planned construct rather than an unplanned contingency. Together, this pair of master tropes constitutes the dynamic of hypertext discourse: the dialectic between searching and finding typical of games in general. The aporia-epiphany pair is thus not a narrative structure but constitutes a more fundamental layer of human experience, from which narratives are spun.

Again, probably the best example of this in *Afternoon* can be found in Douglas's account of her readings, which constitutes a narrative version (almost an adaptation) of the hypertext in a way denied to the hypertext itself. Here, Douglas relates the progress of four reading attempts, the first of which ends abruptly at the place "I call": "the text will not default and I can physically proceed no further without altering my reading strategy" (1994, 166). The second and third readings raise several other questions about the events, but by the fourth reading, because her previous excursions to other parts of the text have released the "guard fields" that barred the way, she manages to penetrate into what for her becomes the heart of *Afternoon*, the place called "white afternoon," where she learns of what happened to the main character's wife and son. Aporia is replaced by epiphany, and the result is a sated "desire for closure" (172).

The Poetics of Conflict: Ergodics versus Narration

What is the structural relationship between *Afternoon* and a typical modernist codex text? In a traditional, Aristotelian narrative, the relationship between author, narrator, narratee, and reader can be portrayed by a communication model shown in figure 4.2. The author puts the words into the mouth of a fictional narrator, who addresses a narratee with whom the real reader identifies. In modernist fiction, such as the novels of Samuel Beckett, there is often a distance between the narrator and narratee, a monologic stream of words that does not seem to reach an intended listener; see figure 4.3.

In *Afternoon*, however, the communication between narrator and narratee works well; the dialogues and monologues within each screen appear to make sense, and the parts of the text we can observe appear to be fragments of some (fairly) rational narrative see figure 4.4). But the relationships between author and narrator, and narratee and reader, seem to be in trouble. As the reader jumps dis-

Figure 4.2. A Communication Model of Classical Narrative

Figure 4.3. Communication in Modernist Fiction

Figure 4.4. Communication Discontinuity in *Afternoon*

continuously between the narrative strands, the story seems to slip away and lose focus, as if someone wanted to sabotage the possibility of narrative progress and the reader's identification with the narratee. And while the narrator is making perfect sense to the narratee within every fragment, the disordered state of the fragments disrupts the narrator's effort, as if there were an "other"—an anti-narrator—who constantly derails and distracts the narrative. This other may or may not be the author, but he or she is at least as powerful as the author and more powerful than the narrator.

Is *Afternoon* a narrative? There are certainly narrative elements in the text working to achieve coherence and meaning, but there is also an opposite force, a destabilizing disfiguration that bears down on the reader's patience and sense of progress. To counter this anti-hermeneutic circle, the reader has to become a metareader, mapping the network and reading the map of her own reading carefully. This is not interactivity (understood as Andrew Lippman's "mutual and simultaneous activity on the part of both participants"; see Brand 1988, 46) but a strategic counterattack upon the limited role or perspective offered to the reader by the hermetic text and an effort to regain a sense of readership. To suggest that the reader is a reader-author is to deny that the gap between these two positions has never been greater. If there is satisfaction, as in Douglas's model reading, it means simply that the would-be reader has managed to become a reader-reader, also in the sense of reading herself. Readership has been restored but not transcended.

We might label *Afternoon* a *reluctant narrative,* or an *antinarrative,* or a *sabotaged narrative,* terms typical of modernist poetics. But perhaps the best descriptive term for *Afternoon* is *game of narration.* If we accept that narration can take place without narrative (as defined by the narratologists), we might come up with a better concept than weak and negatory terms such as *antistory* and *non-linear narrative. Afternoon* is not an antinarrative; it is something other than narrative. As we saw in the previous section, the aporia-epiphany structure is not a narrative device, although it willingly generates narratives when experienced. So what is it? There is a tendency in much cultural theory to posit narrative as the grand structure of everything, the foundation upon which we order our lives and actions. To suggest that narrative is not wholly deserving of this reverence might be risky, since it is all too easy to point out that even the very point I am making here could not be made without the support of narrative. But the story of an event is not necessarily the same as the event itself, and stories can be told about things other than stories, luckily. Furthermore, there is no reason that the basic elements of narrative cannot be used for other purposes. For instance, both stories and games of football consist of a succession of events. But even though stories might be told about it, a foot-ball match is not in itself a story. The actions within the game are not narrative actions. So what are they? The adjective I propose for this function is *ergodic,* which implies a situation in which a chain of events (a path, a sequence of actions, etc.) has been produced by the nontrivial efforts of one or more individuals or mechanisms (see chap. 1).

If we concur with Gérard Genette's claim that narratives comprise two kinds of representations, description and narration, and that description ("The house is white, with a slate roof and green shutters") is always subordinate to narration ("The man went over to the table and picked up a knife"; Genette 1982, 133–34), then we may conceptualize the difference between narratives, games, and hypertexts as follows. Narratives have two levels, description and narration. A game such as football has one level, the ergodic. A video game (e.g., Atari's *Pac-Man*) has description (the screen icons) and ergodics (the forced succession of events) but not narration (the game may be narrated in a number of ways, but like football, narration is not part of the game). A hypertext such as *Afternoon* has all three: description ("Her face was a mirror"), narration ("I call Lolly"), and ergodics (the reader's choices). Unresolved here, and what makes *Afternoon* special as the most accomplished of its kind, is the conflict between narration and ergodics, between narrative and game. This is a border conflict, which is not found (or is at least much less prominent) in hypertexts with only description and ergodics, such as an encyclopedia or a user's manual. To make sense of the text, the reader must produce a narrative version of it, but the ergodic experience marks this version with the reader's signature, the proof that *Afternoon* does not contain a narrative of its own.

Transclusions

This chapter is devoted to contructing a viable terminology for the critical understanding of literary hypertext, showing, via *Afternoon*, how literary hypertext relates to modernism and how the modernist aspects of *Afternoon* dominate the text far more than its postmodernist devices. Hypertext mechanisms are used to achieve effects similar to, but not identical to, the elements of classic modernist novels. The discussion also shows how rhetoric can be used to describe the figures of hypertext discourse and how the master tropes of aporia and epiphany control the progress and rhythm of the reader's investigation. Finally, I question the common labeling of *Afternoon* as a narrative and argue that my concept of ergodic literature might throw some light on the text's unclear status. *Afternoon* is an important limit text, on the border between narrative and ergodics, and may help us understand the limits of the categories of hypertext and narrative, even as it subverts them.

The terms and perspectives developed here, although they were developed with the structures of one specific text in mind, should have relevance to the field of hypertext discourse in general. It is my hope that they stimulate further critical thought both on the special problems of understanding the similarities and differences between hypertext and codex and on the way terms inherited from codex literary theory affect our perceptions in a new field.

Five

Intrigue and Discourse
in the Adventure Game

A Brief History of the Genre

Few literary genres, if any, can be traced to a single point of origin. Does the novel start with Cervantes, Sterne, or the ancient Greeks? What was the first poem? Who wrote the first sonnet? The first detective novel? Most of these questions have no clear answer, and therefore we are not bothered by them. To pinpoint a genre's origin is to define the genre, not to discover it. Hegemonic traditions generally seem to start in some prehistoric time, well before the spotlights of critical attention flooded the scene. In the case of the adventure game, which is the subject of this chapter, an origin can be established, but to do so we must first relate a brief history of the Net, a background also relevant for the history of the *Multi-User Dungeons* discussed in chapter 7.

In these media-infested times, when it is unusual to make a movie without at the same time making a documentary movie about its making, hardly any innovation in the communicative arts goes unnoticed. Among the biggest media events are the media themselves. Since around 1990, the hegemony of the modern mass media have been challenged by the digital network media, most importantly the media of the Internet. The success of this challenge is evident from the attention Internet media are getting from the traditional media. In recent news features, books, movies, art exhibitions, and even the theater, the traditional media pay homage to the Internet like defeated armies throwing their weapons at the feet of the victor. It becomes increasingly harder to remember what life was like before the Net, just as it became harder for our parents to remember life before television.

The Internet seems to have been around longer than one might think: it is usually traced back to 1969, when the first nodes of the ARPANET were made operable (see Spilling 1995). But the ARPANET, connecting a dozen, later some hundred, military and research organizations in the United States, was not the Internet, only a predecessor with a much narrower social, economic, and organizational structure. In 1975, a technical network protocol was introduced that was capable of interconnecting different network technologies. In 1983, as the ARPANET was modernized with the new, flexible internet protocol (IP) and as independent organizations were allowed to connect, *Internet* became the new name of the network. It was still under the supervision of the U.S. Department of Defense Advanced Research Projects Agency (DARPA). By 1987, when new infrastructure had rendered the old ARPANET superfluous, DARPA closed the Internet project and gave up control, leaving the growing conglomerate of independent networks to its own uncontrolled and exponential growth. This was what years later became widely known as the Internet, but in those days it was usually referred to as the Net. In popular computer magazines of the late 1980s, the Internet is usually not mentioned, not even in articles on the subject of electronic mail. The idea (and ideology) of the Internet seems to have crystallized around 1988–89, when the number of users reached the critical mass sufficient to catch the interest of the mass media, helped by such major events as the "Internet worm" incident in November 1988, when a young computer hacker released a self-spreading program that paralyzed thousands of Internet machines (see Hafner and Markoff 1991).

But more than twelve years before the Internet worm, a different, though some say equally productivity threatening, computer program was released over the ARPANET. In the mid-1970s, programer William Crowther got the idea that a game similar to Gary Gygax's popular role-playing board game, *Dungeons and Dragons,* could be made and played on a computer (Crowther and Woods 1976; Gygax 1974). In Gygax's strategy board game and its many descendants, a group of adventurers explore a two-dimensional fantasy world controlled, improvised, and sometimes created by a dungeon master (DM). The players choose among the options laid out by the DM and roll dice to settle the outcome of battles between opponents and DM-controlled monsters. The *Dungeons and Dragons* genre might be regarded as an oral cybertext, the oral predecessor to computerized, written, adventure games.

Here is Don Woods' account of how he and Crowther developed the first *Adventure* game:

> Crowther, who is also an avid caver (the caver's term for a spelunker), decided to try writing a program to simulate cave exploration. He added some treasures and hostile dwarves to spice it up, but it was mainly just an exploration game. (I believe he intended to extend it into a computer referee for role-playing, but it never got that far.) He called it Adventures (plural). This was sometime in the early 70's.
>
> The Adventures game migrated across the ArpaNet, and I ran into a copy at Stanford during my first year of graduate school (75–76). I thought it was a neat idea for a game, but there wasn't a lot to it, and it was full of bugs. The credits said to direct questions to "Willie Crowther." The net wasn't as big in those days (no Usenet, and "only" a few hundred Arpanet sites), so I sent mail to crowther@xxx for every host xxx on the net. I got back lots of error messages, but eventually did hear from Crowther, who by then was working at Xerox PARC. He sent me the source in return for a promise that I would send him any changes. I called my version Adventure. Because of the limitations on the length and capitalisation of file names, the actual file was called ADVENT.
>
> In April '76 I finished version 1, and made it available via a guest login. Then I left for a vacation. When I got back a week or two later, I found the system administrators were annoyed because of the heavy system load caused by people logging in from all over the net to play Adventure.
>
> That summer I touched up a few things, like adding scoring and the endgame, and a "wizard mode" that let me set up limits on the times when it would let people play. Then I began sending source copies to anyone who wanted one. And it proceeded to turn up all over the world. (Woods, personal correspondence with author, September 29, 1993)

This autobiographical origin story of Crowther and Woods' *Adventure* is a paradigm of collaborative authorship on the Net: one person gets an idea, writes a program, releases it (with the source code); somewhere else another person picks it up, improves it, adds new ideas, and rereleases it. Most of the time they do not meet face to face. Mary Ann Buckles (1985, 79) argues convincingly that *Adventure* can be classified as "folk art," in contrast to the popular commercial genre it later gave birth to.

After Woods' version was released in 1976, the game became immensely successful. In addition to inaugurating the genre, which for a while was the most popular type of computer game, it inspired a host of new media types and literary experiments, from the hypertext novels to "interactive" pornography on CD-ROM. With the explosive growth in the home computer market around 1975–80, a market for computer games had suddenly appeared, and the adventure game structure, much simpler to program than graphic arcade games, was easy to exploit and package for this market. In 1978, Scott Adams and his new company Adventure International produced the first adventure game for a microcomputer, *Adventureland*, for the TRS-80.

The formula was simple: take a popular fiction genre, for example, the detective novel, create a background story (the more stereotypical the better, since the players would need less initiation), create a map for the player to move around in, objects to manipulate, characters to interact with, a plot tree or graph with several outcomes, depending on the player's previous decisions, and add descriptions, dialogue, error messages, and a vocabulary for the player. This literary database is accessed via a subprogram called a *parser* that interprets the player's input commands (e.g., hit dragon, eat sandwich, go north). Once an action has been identified, the program changes the database and displays a message about the outcome, until the player quits the game, wins, or "dies" and must start again.

Once the parser and database tools have been developed, these can be reused for several games, and game development then becomes much like planning and writing a piece of short fiction, except that multiple outcomes must be conceived and the player's actions (however unreasonable) must be predicted. Since the source code for *Adventure* was available, many game developers simply ported it to any new computer that came along. Creating a version is mainly a matter of editing and then recompiling a program file; the end result can be as similar or different from the original as the programer wants. Some developers were little more than epigones, copying both the techniques and the theme, others used the same techniques but for different themes, and yet others improved both the techniques and themes considerably.

Among the most influential of the early adventure game companies was Infocom, which consisted of a group of programers from MIT's AI lab. Infocom's first game, *Zork* (written in 1977), by Marc Blank and Dave Lebling, was similar to Crowther and Woods' original in setting (an underground empire) but was better at parsing and world simulation. Blank and Lebling created a series of accomplished, now classic, adventure games, starting with the *Zork* trilogy (published 1980–82) and ranging from the burlesque (*Leather Goddesses of Phobos* [1986], by Steve Meretzky) to the contemplative (*A Mind Forever Voyaging* [1985], also by Meretzky). For a while, the genre thrived, especially in Anglo-American cultures, with dedicated monthly magazines, notably the British *Micro Adventurer*, do-it-yourself books, and numerous games developed by amateurs and professionals. Adaptations of popular literature, such as Arthur Conan Doyle's Sherlock Holmes novels, J. R. R. Tolkien's *The Hobbit* and *The Lord of the Rings*, and Douglas Adams' *The Hitch-Hiker's Guide to the Galaxy*, were published alongside generic crime, science fiction, and fantasy productions.[1] Today, however, the textual adventure game is no longer popular. It achieved a short but considerable success (*Zork* is said to have sold a million copies), which ended quietly in the late 1980s, when the public lost interest and game companies stopped production. Perhaps the beginning of the end was Activision's takeover of Infocom in 1986, which was followed by regular annual losses until its complete shutdown in 1989.

A history of this remarkable, short-lived genre would of course be incomplete without an attempt to explain its demise. According to Brenda Laurel (1991, 97n), the first graphical adventure game was created by Warren Robinett for Atari in 1979. In the early 1980s, computer graphics became better and cheaper, and so the adventure game genre, with its spatially oriented themes of travel and

1. For an extensive and very useful gameography of the adventure game genre, see Hans Persson (1995).

discovery, gradually migrated from text to pictures and, eventually, to three-dimensional "virtual reality" games like *Doom*, by John Romero, John Carmack, and Adrian Carmack (1993), or multipath movies like the current Hollywood CD-ROM productions. It is not entirely correct to say that the *Doom*-type game, unlike the multipath movies, is a direct descendant of *Adventure*. There is another type of game—in some ways closer to the noncomputerized *Dungeons and Dragons*, which inspired them all—that has had at least as much influence on the three-dimensional action games, and that is the two-dimensional, ASCII-character matrix game *Rogue*, created by Michael Toy, Glenn Wichman, and Ken Arnold in 1980. *Rogue* pioneered the graphical, multilevel, discover-as-you-go labyrinth dungeon, had real time action (monster fighting), and inspired a host of similar games, which eventually moved from the crude ASCII representation (the player was represented with an @) to the bit maps, vector graphics, and polygon engines that are standard today. But since *Adventure* was created four years earlier than *Rogue*, it is reasonable to assume that the *Rogue* tradition was also strongly inspired by the adventure games.

Images, especially moving images, are more powerful representations of spatial relations than texts, and therefore this migration from text to graphics is natural and inevitable. And in the meantime, adventure games had inspired other text genres, such as multi-user dungeons, where the relations between users and producers really are interactive and equal; and hypertext novels, where "literary" ideals and ambitions are much easier to fulfill, since the reader's level of involvement is much closer to that of traditional fiction. There is also an active, noncommercial movement on the Internet that cultivates the traditional adventure game structure and continues to create free or shareware adventure games (see the Usenet group rec.arts.int-fiction and the ftp archive at ftp.gmd.de.). Despite this creative and vigorous community, however, the chances for a popular revival of the textual adventure game seem less than promising at this moment.

But the ergodic structures invented by Crowther and Woods twenty years ago are of course far from dead but instead persevere as the basic figure for the large and growing industrial entertainment genre called, by a somewhat catachresic pleonasm, "interactive games." (A game with fixed paths and choices is much less interactive than a game with goal-oriented, flexible opponents. If these games are interactive, what game isn't? Here, as elsewhere, *interactive* is just another word for computerized.) It is a paradox that, despite the lavish and quite expensive graphics of these productions, the player's creative options are still as primitive as they were in 1976.

A Schematic Model of Internal Structure

Although a discussion of adventure games and similar systems would be incomplete without a description of the internal mimetic machine, it will be examined only briefly here. Partly because different types of cybertexts have very different mechanical structures (or algorithms), I want to avoid technical detail. This is, after all, not a comparative study of cybertext programing methods. The model presented here does not represent any particular cybertext system, nor does it pretend to describe all features shared by all such systems. It is not a realistic model, with a one-to-one mapping of actual components. It should instead be seen as a generalized conceptualization of the functionality of a typical, but advanced, adventure game.

The internal design of cybertexts has come a long way since the original *Adventure*, which "required about 300K of computer memory to play" (Gerrard 1984, 3). Later, more advanced cybertexts have managed on a lot less, catering to the limitations of the early home computers. With the development of *Zork* came the idea of an adventure interpreter (the Z-machine, in Infocom's case), an independent program module that could be used in more than one cybertext, like a database engine for several databases. Later, several specialized computer languages for cybertext construction appeared, such as Graham Nelson's Z-machine-compatible compiler, Inform, and also more high-level construction systems that did not require programing skills, such as Bill Appleton's World Builder.

In figure 5.1, the "ideal components" and information flow (arrows) of a cybertext is shown. The model is not limited to single-user adventure games or text-based games but can also describe

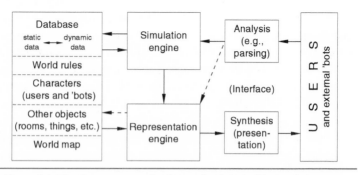

Figure 5.1. The Components of a Generalized, Role-Playing Cybertext

multi-user dungeons and graphical games such as *Doom*. Notice the four groups of components: the data, the processing engines, the front-end medium (interface), and the users; and note the way information flows in feedback loops among them: going left on the upper level and then right on the lower, with the two middle layers like an artificial heart pumping information between the user and the database. This model is best suited to describe indeterminate cybertext. In determinate cybertext (e.g., *Adventure*), the three functions—simulation, representation, and synthesis—might be better described as a single component.

In the first of the four functional layers (the database), the data is of two kinds, static or dynamic. Some cybertexts, especially the early ones, had mostly static information, with only a few dynamic data items (the variables containing the position and status of the user's character and a few other objects), while the rest (topology, descriptions, the other characters' behavior) was read-only. Contradistinctively, in a multi-user dungeon, there are in principle no static data, although the basic topology (e.g., the links between the most common "rooms") tends to remain unchanged.

The second layer, the processing engines, represents the core of the cybertext. In the simulation engine, the course of action is decided, based on the user's input, the cybertext's idiosyncratic rules, and the current state of the simulated world. Here the events of the simulation are calculated and passed on to the representation engine. There can be two types of events: the ones generated by user input (user events) and those generated by the simulation itself (system events), normally caused by certain conditions coming true, for example, the passing of a specified period of time. Typically, the early adventure games were driven by user events only, and time was measured by counting the number of user moves. If the user did nothing, time stood still.

The representation engine presents the results of the event to the user by providing a personal perspective on the simulated world. It shows only those events that directly relate to the user's character and its surroundings, such as actions observed by, or participated in, by the user's character. In a user-configurative cybertext, the representation engine also handles the user's configurative commands (the dashed arrows), such as changing information "owned" by the user (e.g., the user's character's description).

The third layer, commonly known as the interface, consists of an input and an output component. The input component analyzes the user's commands and translates them into a semantic code that can be digested by the simulation engine. The type of input component depends on the channel, which can be text, static graphics, a combination of these two, or sound and animated graphics. The same is true of the output component, which transforms the semantic information it gets from the representation engine into the type of expression specified by the channel.

There is an obvious benefit in keeping the data base layer separate from the processing layer and this again separate from the input-output layer: when better technologies arrive, an individual component can be replaced without major changes in the others.

The fourth layer of the model, the user, is of course external to the design of the cybertext but not to its strategy. In the early adventure games, this strategy assumed an ideal reader, who would solve all the riddles of the text and thereby extricate the one definite, intended plotline. Eventually, this strategy changed, and now the reader's role is becoming less ideal (both in a structural and a moral sense) and more flexible, less dependable (hence more responsible), and freer. The multiuser, programable cybertext instigates a more worldwise, corruptible reader; a Faust, compared to the Sherlock Holmes of the early adventure games.

Some Issues in Adventure Game Criticism

There are many ways for critics to focus the adventure game genre. From a postmodernist perspective, where the boredom with the current literary experiments carried over from modernism is hardly concealable,[2] the ludic possibilities of new media positions are sometimes idealized beyond recognition. Linda Hutcheon, in a discussion of postmodern art's focus on its own production, posits "interactive fiction" as the "most extreme example I can think of in art. . . . Here process is all; there is no fixed product or text, just the reader's activity as producer as well as receiver" (1988, 77). The claim that adventure games consist of nothing but "the reader's activity" is clearly false; otherwise they could hardly be discussed at all. Hutcheon's misrepresentation is understandable in light of the often self-contradictory Anthony Niesz and Norman N. Holland article she refers to, where it is claimed that, in interactive fiction, "in a literal sense, there is *no* text, nothing that could be put on a shelf and pointed to as the source of roughly similar experiences by readers" (1984, 120). Later in the article they reverse the claim: "Both interactive and traditional fiction rely upon the use of written texts, or upon the elements of narration, plot, and dialogue" (125). In most adventure game situations, the reader's activity is very predictable. Certainly it is fair to say that it is being produced or directed by the text, within the limited freedom of the available commands.

Two of the most common approaches to adventure games seem to be apologetics and trivialization. Both generally fail to grasp the intrinsic qualities of the genre, because they both privilege the aesthetic ideals of another genre, that of narrative literature, typically the novel. For the apologists, adventure games may one day—when their Cervantes or Dickens comes along—reach their true potential, produce works of literary value that rival the current narrative masterpieces, and claim their place in the canon. For the trivialists, this will never happen; adventure games are games—they can-

2. See Frederic Jameson (1991, 298), commenting on postmodern art: "The music is not bad to listen to, or the poetry to read; the [high literary] novel is the weakest of the newer cultural areas and is considerably excelled by its narrative counterparts in film and video."

not possibly be taken seriously as literature nor attain the level of sophistication of a good novel. Although the trivialists are right—adventure games will never become good novels—they are also making an irrelevant point, because adventure games are not novels at all. The adventure game is an artistic genre of its own, a unique aesthetic field of possibilities, which must be judged on its own terms. And while the apologists certainly are wrong, in that the games will never be considered good novels, they are right in insisting that the genre may improve and eventually turn out something rich and wonderful. This may or may not happen, so the only way to understand the genre is to study the various works that already exist and how they are played.

Over the last decade or so, a number of studies have addressed the adventure game as a literary genre—or at least has discussed them from a perspective of literary theory and criticism. The distinction here is important, because while the critics apply or suggest literary perspectives, they do not always treat the adventure games as they would a literary work. Even Buckles, in her interesting dissertation devoted to the "storygame" *Adventure* (1985), seems uninterested in placing her subject text at a specific point in history, and she mentions its creators, Crowther and Woods, only in footnotes (e.g., 24, n. 2). Most commentators and critics of the adventure game genre (Bolter and Joyce 1987; Randall 1988; Ziegfeld 1989; Bolter 1991; Sloane 1991; Murray 1995) fail to mention the original *Adventure* at all, and those who do usually date it far off the mark (Niesz and Holland 1984; Lanestedt 1989; Aarseth 1994) and often neglect to mention its creators (Moulthrop and Kaplan 1991; Kelley 1993). In contrast, contemporary journalism at least got the time and places right: "The first participatory computer tale, *Adventure*, was created in the mid-1970s by computer researchers in Cambridge and Stanford" (Elmer–De Witt and Murphy 1983).

Why this neglect? A trivial answer would be, because none of these critics seem to have felt much need for historical perspectives. Hence, in the tradition of adventure game criticism the origin of the genre just never became an issue. But I suspect the main reason is that we are dealing with the first instance of a new type of literary artifact. *Adventure*, despite its obvious debt to *Dungeons and Drag-*

ons, transcended the cultural position of a singular text and became a mythological urtext, located everywhere and nowhere, sometimes even incorrectly backdated to the early sixties. Thus we have, ironically, a situation apparently not unlike that facing researchers of early literary history, where author attributions, version causality, and publication dates are in question. One can only imagine what the proponents of "electronic writing" as a type of "secondary orality" might make of this. But the situation would easily have been avoided if a few of these critics had shown a minimum of historical curiosity and had investigated the matter.

Alternative reasons could be that, unlike *Zork*—which is often, and undeservingly, claimed as the paradigmatic adventure game— *Adventure* was not sold and marketed under a single name by named authors and a specific publisher but rather gave birth to numerous imitations and mutations while it led a parallel existence as a game file on central computers all over the academic and computer-industrial world. The critics, perhaps unfamiliar with the sources of free software, simply might not have found it listed in commercial game catalogs. Some might argue that it does not display the level of literary sophistication achieved by later hallmarks in the genre and is, therefore, unworthy of critical attention. But this last option is not correct, as Buckles' extensive analysis shows.[3] Buckles does state that *Adventure* "is of low literary quality" (1985, 82), but this judgment seems refuted by her own rich and attentive account of its pioneering aspects and especially by her fascinating observations of the variation in strategy and response from player to player. *Adventure* contains many artistic qualities, and in that respect far surpasses many ensuing works, such as Scott Adams' *Adventureland,* where descriptions are kept at an absolute minimum.

Attempts to apply the perspectives of literary theory to the adventure game genre have been sparse and unconcerted. Over the last decade, since Niesz and Holland's 1984 article, several individual attempts have been made to put the genre on the agenda of literary studies, but perhaps understandably, no breakthrough has

---

3. For a long discussion of *Adventure,* see Mary Ann Buckles (1985). For a short taste, see Espen Aarseth (1994, 73).

yet been made. As the Hutcheon quotation above illustrates, the games have remained a curiosity, an "extreme example." The much younger genre of hypertext literature has been much more successful in this respect, for several reasons: the eloquent way in which their practitioners and commentators have associated them with the theoretical vogues of postmodernism and poststructuralism; their more "serious" written content; and most of all, their discourse format, which is clearly recognizable as experimental literature, which is more commodifiable in university literature departments than game programs and clearly akin to already canonized modernist and postmodernist texts. Adventure games, despite some of their authors' growing "concern for the literariness of their product" (Randall 1988, 183), are simply too different and too easily identified as "entertainment" (correctly, but irrelevantly) to be eligible for scholarly attention from literary theory and criticism. Compared to all other literary formats, including hypertext novels, the adventure game's textual structure is an alien, too far removed from the genus of hegemonic literature to be recognized by any but a few xenophiles, who risk professional suspicion or ridicule when they dare suggest the pertinence of their newfound, strange looking object. No wonder their chosen strategy most often is one of seeking similarity, bridging the gap, and trying to find a perspective, however narrow, that demonstrates that the species does not lack all the important marks of literature that we know and love so well.

But this construction of similarity is of limited potential, since the most interesting feature of these texts are their difference from, and not their (inferior) resemblance to, the hegemonic forms. What above all makes them worthy of study is the fact that they present an alternative mode of discourse; a different type of textual pleasure. By investigating this we may be able to extract knowledge of a more general kind, which may tell us something about discourse itself and which we could not have learned from our previous, more restricted horizon. This is sufficient reason to put the adventure game on the agenda of literary study, in agreement with the ideals of comparative literature.

To date, the most varied, thorough, and valuable contribution to adventure game theory remains Buckles' 1985 dissertation, despite its somewhat long-winded arguments and use of sometimes less than rigorous terminology (e.g., "story"). Many of the aesthetic issues she introduces, such as the problem of creating "nonstereotype, subtle characters" (82), are even more relevant today, when computer games seem dominated by either completely robotic villains (such as the nonplaying characters in *Doom*) or completely unpopulated (and therefore, in my opinion), utterly boring spaces (*Myst*). Buckles focuses her attention on *Adventure* and compares it critically to folktales and the first printed quest novels, using Vladimir Propp's *Morphology of the Folk Tale*. She also employs a rich set of other perspectives, among them theories of popular literature, observations of and interviews with actual players, and a combinatorial analysis of the game's potential for variation of output.

Among the other themes engaged by the literary theorists and critics of adventure games have been the literariness of game authors' strategies in light of Viktor Shklovskij's concept of *ostranenie*, or strangeness (Randall 1988); whether adventure games are media for literary storytelling, by way of Jonathan Culler's structuralist poetics (Lanestedt 1989); whether this is "a new literary genre" (Ziegfeld 1989); the inadequacy of the standard communication model ("the rhetorical triangle") to describe adventure game play (Sloane 1991); and the internal conflict between Barthesian "readerly" and "writerly" textuality (Kelley 1993).

A recurrent issue is the central notion of reader response theory of *leerstellen*—blanks, gaps (Iser 1974, 1978). From the point of view of adventure-game-as-story (which I do not subscribe to), the user's participation is a filling in of the gaps in the narrative provided by the text. This has led a number of critics—Anthony Niesz and Norman Holland (1984), Mary Ann Buckles (1985, 1987), Neil Randall (1988), Richard Ziegfeld (1989), Jon Lanestedt (1989), and Sarah Jane Sloane (1991)—to point to Wolfgang Iser's theory of literary *leerstellen*, the semantic gaps in the text that the reader must fill, to bring "the literary work into existence" (Iser 1980, 50). They all argue that the adventure game has a second type of gap, a narrative vacancy, which must be filled by the reader for the "text" to continue.

There can be little doubt that Iser's theory is as relevant for cybertext as it is for any other kind of literature. Adventure games depend on their reader's mental involvement in order to realize what Iser calls the aesthetic pole of the literary work. But the theoretical figure of gaps can be misleading when used to describe how adventure games are different—and not only because of Iser's distinctive sense of the term. There is, as Buckles notes, a crucial difference between Iser's aesthetic gaps and what she and others see as the narrative gaps of determinate cybertext, a difference that goes beyond the mere physical difference in the reader's response.

The "openings" of determinate cybertexts are not gaps, in Iser's sense, since they are not used to complement the written parts in a game of imagination; rather, they are used as a filter, in which only the "correct" response lets the user proceed through the text. To use another metaphor, they are keyholes, fitted by the text for very specific keys. However, even if the key fits (i.e., the command, such as open the balcony door, is successfully executed), the strategic progression of the game may not be affected at all. The openings, or keyholes, of the adventure game are therefore of two different functional kinds: those that advance the strategic position of the player and those that don't. Only the first are gaps in the quest for the solution of the game, but on a "narrative" level there is no discernible difference. This suggests that what Buckles and others see as a type of narrative gap is in fact not a narrative phenomenon but is related to the game's structure in a fundamentally different way. Furthermore, it seems to suggest that the standard concepts of narratology are not sufficient to explain the literary phenomena of adventure games, and certainly not their difference from other types of literature. In the next section I introduce some alternative concepts with which we may begin to examine the texts that have been obscured by the shadow of narrative and its powerful theories for too long.

Intrigue, Intrigant, Intriguee

For Iser, the story of a narrative is produced by a "convergence of text and reader" (1980, 50), a process in which the reader enriches the "literary work" by interaction with the plot. In the adventure game or determinate cybertext, far from moving toward a story by means of a plot with significant gaps, it is the plot that is narrowed down, by a designifying of the gaps. From many potential stories, a single plot is extracted (if the player is successful).

In the determinate cybertext, then, the functions of plot (*sjuzet*) and story (*fabula*) appear to have traded places, somehow. But this is not exactly the case. The concept of plot is unsettled by the reader (user), who, being strategically within it, is in no position to see through it and glimpse a story behind. It is often argued that narrative plot is also something that is only discovered or reconstructed by the reader after the end is reached; and this could be seen to imply, contrary to my argument, that there is no great difference between the narrative and the ergodic situation as far as plot is concerned. But there is a difference, and for a very simple reason: the bewildered reader of a narrative can safely assume that the events that are already encountered, however mystifying, will make sense in the end (if the plot is to make sense at all); whereas the player of an adventure game (*Deadline* is a good example) is not guaranteed that the events thus far are at all relevant to the solution of the game.

Hence it could be argued that the reader *is* (or at least produces) the story. A more moderate proposition is that there is no story at all, in the traditional sense. Contrary to Niesz and Holland's claim, that the adventure game "does no more than introduce an extra stage" (1984, 125), I argue that it effectively disintegrates any notion of story by forcing the player's attention on the elusive "plot." Instead of a narrated plot, cybertext produces a sequence of oscillating activities effectuated (but certainly not controlled) by the user. But there is nevertheless a structuring element in these texts, which in some way does the controlling or at least motivates it. As a new term for this element I propose *intrigue*, to suggest a secret plot in which the user is the innocent, but voluntary, target (*victim* is too strong a term), with an outcome that is not yet decided—or rather with several possible outcomes that depend on various factors, such as the cleverness and experience of the player. The term *intrigue* is of course borrowed from drama theory, where it refers to "a scheme which depends for its success on the ignorance or gullibility of the person or persons against whom it is directed" (Abrams 1981, 137). The difference between dramatic intrigue and ergodic intrigue is that the dramatic intrigue takes place on a diegetic, intrafictional level as a plot within the plot and, usually, with the audience's full knowledge, while ergodic intrigue is directed against the user, who must figure out for herself what is going on. Also, ergodic intrigue must have more than one explicit outcome and cannot, therefore, be successful or unsuccessful; this attribute here depends on the player.

The target of the intrigue might be called the *intriguee* and is a parallel to the narratee, to the implied reader of the narratologists, as well as to the main character (or "puppet," as Sloane calls it). As I argue elsewhere, the distance between these three positions collapses in the adventure game: the user assumes the role of the main character and, therefore, will not come to see this person as an other, or as a person at all, but rather as a remote-controlled extension of herself. The narratee (or perhaps simply addressee) likewise is subsumed in this identification process. On the other hand, the difference between the three positions still exists as an epistemological hierarchy, best seen through the event of the main character's death. "The main character is simply dead, erased, and must begin again. The narratee, on the other hand, is explicitly told what happened, usually in a sarcastic manner, and offered the chance to start anew. The user, aware of all this in a way denied to the narratee, learns from the mistakes and previous experience and is able to play a different game" (Aarseth 1994, 73–74).

The position of the intriguee is transcendental, as it depends on the strategic identification or merger between the player and the puppet. When the game is over, and the player is either satisfied (aware of the game's secrets) or too frustrated to play any more, this union dissolves, along with the motivation to play. Niesz and Holland see this drop in interest as a sign that adventure games are trivial, "like pop fiction, read once and no more" (1984, 122), but this comparison is faulty, since the efforts and time spent solving an adventure game typically are much more similar to, say, reading and rereading a difficult novel, than leafing through a page-turner once. As Buckles (1985, 185) observes in her critique of Niesz and Holland, adventure games have "a strong contemplative quality" that these authors seem to overlook. A typical adventure game is not mastered by being "read" once but by being played over and over, as the way we reread a great and complex novel. In both cases, when we feel that there is nothing more to be discovered, we eventually lose interest.

Intrigue is not locatable on any particular level of the text, or as a separate module, but it may be surmised from the overall construction and by playing. Intrigue is parallel to Seymour Chatman's concept of story, the *what* that is transmitted by the text, rather than the *way* ("the *how*") it is transmitted. Like Chatman's story, intrigue contains what he calls events (actions and happenings) and existents (characters and settings; see Chatman 1978, 19), but here these ingredients are not connected in a fixed sequence. Instead of the linear structure that Chatman calls the "event dimension" (42) of the narrative, intrigue constitutes a multidimensional event space and unfolds through the negotiation of this space by text and user. This unfolding brings to mind the concept of a log, a recording of a series of experienced events. Thus the determinate cybertext reconfigures literary experience along a different plane than the narrative. Instead of a narrative constituted of a story or plot, we get an intrigue-oriented ergodic log—or to adopt Gérard Genette's (1980) and Seymour Chatman's (1978) term, ergodic *discourse.*

As a corollary to the intriguee, there is the intrigant, the intrigue's alternative to the narrative's narrator. Here it may be objected that the adventure game already has a narrator, and in a linguistic sense this is true. Between the intrigant and the intriguee we have what may be called the game's voice, the simulated correspondent that relates events to the implied user. This voice is not functionally identical to the various types of narrators that we observe in narrative fiction, since the ergodic voice is both more (a negotiator) and less (a mechanical construct in a real sense) than the teller of a tale. The intrigant, as the architect of the intrigue, might instead be compared to an implied author, the mastermind who is ultimately responsible for events and existents but who is not motivated by a particular outcom. But as we shall see, this comparison has its limitations.

The Autistic Detective Agency: Marc Blank's *Deadline*

Marc Blank's *Deadline* (1982), published by Infocom, is a classic from the golden age of adventure games, just after the genre's establishment as a successful new textual medium and well before its commercial decline due to the migration to graphics. *Deadline* is a traditional detective mystery adapted to adventure game format: a mansion, a murder, and the usual suspects. It differs from the episodic paradigm of treasure hunt, bewildering maze, and tough monsters introduced by *Adventure* and instead confines the action to a closed, limited space (some 50 locations, compared to *Adventure*'s 140) with almost no hidden rooms, no mazes, less than fifteen, all human, characters (if human is the right word), and an intratextual time span of twelve hours.

As the investigating inspector, it is up to you—the player's character (the puppet)—to find out what happened to Marshall Robner, the wealthy businessman who was found dead on the floor of his library. In the house live his wife, Leslie, his black-sheepish son, George, and his thirty-something secretary, Ms. Dunbar. There are two servants, the gossipy housekeeper, Mrs. Rourke, and the rose-obsessed gardener, Mr. McNabb. In addition, there is the family lawyer, Mr. Coates; Mrs. Robner's secret lover, Steven; and a junior business associate, Mr. Baxter. To assist you is trusty Police Sergeant Duffy, and to breathe down your neck is the pushy Chief Inspector Klutz, who won't even let you work overtime to solve the murder but takes you off the case at precisely 8:00 P.M., after only twelve hours at the scene (hence the title of the game). The time passes by a minute each move you make, and you may also wait for specific times or events (e.g., "wait for mcnabb"). When you feel you have uncovered enough evidence, you arrest the suspected murderer.

Personal relations and habits in an adventure game like *Deadline* might best be described as autistic. The *Encyclopaedia Britannica* defines *autism* as "a neurobiological disorder that affects physical, social, and language skills." Further, "it may be characterized by meaningless, noncontextual echolalia (constant repetition of what is said by others) or the replacement of speech by strange mechanical sounds. Inappropriate attachment to objects may occur. There may be underemphasized reaction to sound, no reaction to pain, or no recognition of genuine danger, yet autistic children are extremely sensitive" (*Britannica Online*, "Autism").

The characters you meet in *Deadline* appear to be living in their own private worlds. When questioned, they often repeat themselves without making sense, and you may stand next to them for hours without any sign that they know you are there. Intelligent conversation is exceedingly difficult and breaks down after at most a few exchanges. And your own behavioral range is not much better, as you try to guess the word combinations that will unlock the mystery. Even moving around in the house or garden can be a pain, as the very limited commands for movement (south, west, northwest, up, etc.) will not always get you where you want to go. Most random words you try to use will result in rebuttals.

PLAYER: Stroll around.
VOICE: The word "stroll" isn't in your vocabulary.
PLAYER: Go for a walk.
VOICE: The word " 'walk" can't be used in that sense.

Sometimes the answers are pure nonsense:

PLAYER: Fingerprint me.
VOICE: Upon looking over and dusting the me you notice that there are no good fingerprints to be found.
PLAYER: Talk to Duffy.
VOICE: You can't talk to the Duffy!

As for "inappropriate attachment to objects," to solve an adventure game, you must collect and examine as many objects as possible, because you never know what you might need later. In *Adventure*, most objects have a function, while in *Deadline*, only six objects are needed to solve the case (unless we count Sergeant Duffy as an object, as the game apparently does). In case of violence (e.g., when the detective is shot by the murderer), the pain of your character means nothing to the player, and it/you may die suddenly before you have recognized the danger. And yet, since solving an adventure game is usually very difficult, it requires extreme sensitivity to details. The contract between user and text in "interactive fiction" is not merely a "willing suspension of disbelief" but a willing suspension of one's normal capacity for language, physical aptness, and social interaction as well. It is of course not autism in a clinical, or even a fictional sense, but functionally it seems very close.

In her reading of *Deadline*, Sloane (1991, 66) suggests that the adventure game genre is characterized by three main features: "multiple point of view, nonlinearity, and second-person address." While the latter two are unproblematic and characterize all works in the genre, the first one, multiple viewpoint—by which Sloane presumably refers to the distance between the game text and the secondary texts, accompanying materials that Infocom packaged with the game diskette (maps, lab reports, transcripts of interviews, instructions for the player, etc.; see Sloane 1991, 68–69)—strikes me as extrinsic, since additional textual perspectives are not a required ingredient for all games of this kind. (It is rather a clever marketing trick, whereby Infocom made it harder for those with pirate copies to enjoy the game.) Neither is multiple viewpoint an integrated component of the game itself but is, rather, what we might call a set of paratexts, accompanying texts that refer to the game in some way, like the reviews of a theater play or its program brochure. The paratexts are of course not limited to the official Infocom package but may include comments and solutions made by players for each other. A common unofficial paratext is the "walkthru," a step-by-step recipe that contains the solution, and "walks" the user through the game. This is of course cheating, but sometimes it is the only way for a novice player to get to the end of a difficult game.

Following Genette's critique of the concept of point of view (1980, 185f.), we might profit from discussing this problem in his alternative terms of *voice* and *perspective*. The game itself is characterized by a singular perspective, which coincides with the user's symbolic presence in the game. In the case of *Deadline* the perspective is limited to that of the investigating detective, a simulated body who obeys the rules of *Deadline's* simulated world. In a superficial sense, this perspective is what we might call realist, as it contains no fantastic or supernatural elements. There are a few metafictional moments in the game, such as the self-referential book in the living room: "This is a novelization of DEADLINE, a classic work of computer fiction. . . . You start to read it, and it seems oddly familiar, as if you had lived it." Reading the end will depress "you" into committing suicide, and the program quits! This must be one of the more brutal types of metalepsis yet invented, or perhaps *dyslepsis* is a better word for it. But these elements are not representative of *Deadline's* intrigue and merely serve to lighten what can be a frustrating experience for a novice player. However, because of the negotiating nature of the adventure game's discourse, this perspective of "realism" is constantly interrupted by the conflict between intrigue and intriguee in terms of language problems, physical-world problems, and "intriguingly incorrect" behavior— that is, when the player tries to act outside of the intrigue's event space. We might refer to this last type of conflict as pushing the intrigue envelope.

The voice, as the narrating go-between that expedites the user's requests and commands and reports the resulting action, is not a reliable entity and may mess things up for the player because of its limited understanding. In addition, it is tiresomely tireless in repeating itself and often presents its messages with a stinging irony and sarcasm. For instance, in *Deadline*, when the player misspells the command "go upstairs" as "up stairs," the voice suggests, "Perhaps it's time for you to rest." This "mischievous spirit" is the intrigant's irritating, unseen agent among the intriguees, a kind of Puck to the intrigant's Oberon. As a negotiator it often makes mistakes or cracks jokes at the player's expense and is usually less than reliable as the servant of the intrigant. But is it really a person, even a simulated one? After talking to players of *Adventure*, Buckles concludes that their interpretations of who or what the "narrator" (as she calls it) is are too individual to form a consensus. "Whether the narrator should be considered the author's voice, their own mind's voice, the game itself, or some type of character—a witness, a participant, one of the protagonists, or an antagonist—depends in the end on the reader" (1985, 147). It also depends on the game in question, of course, but the diegetic, negotiating voice function is one of the most constant and striking elements in adventure game engineering, so a generalization seems legitimate.

Usually, the voice follows the player's instructions and merely reports the resulting action:

PLAYER: Get teacup and saucer.

VOICE Cup: taken. Saucer: taken.

Or

PLAYER: Analyze teacup for ebullion.

VOICE: Sergeant Duffy walks up as quietly as a mouse. He takes the cup from you. "I'll return soon with the results," he says, and leaves as silently as he entered.

Or again,

PLAYER: Go south.

VOICE: End of hallway.

But even here, the voice's curious mixture of styles is noticeable, to the extent that we might want to describe it as two different voices; the curt, minimalist, camera eye style (or nonnarration) in "Cup: taken," and the direct, covert narration in "Sergeant Duffy walks up as quietly as a mouse." The second voice, typically engaged in the long descriptive passages, relates what are usually called canned sentences—prefabricated scriptons that are identical to their textons, with minimal modification at the time of playing. The first voice is used for the ergodic aspects.

In *Adventure*, the voice does feature an overt personality—an "I" that performs subjective acts, such as reincarnating the player-puppet in a magic ritual including orange smoke! (Buckles 1985, 143),—but the voice in *Deadline* never admits to any self-awareness. Even when the player ask directly "Who are you," the oracular reply is, "That question cannot be answered." Only at one point in the game, at the successful ending, does it use the personal pronoun *we*: "You have solved the case! If you would like, you may see the author's summary of the story. We would advise you to come up with your own first!" If the answer is yes, the "story" that follows is not the events of the successful game session but a retrospective exposition, the synopsis of the events that took place before the action began: why Robner was murdered, how, by whom. This "we," coming as it does at the successful end of the intrigue, and referring to "the author" in the third person, seems, if anything, to be coming directly from the (implied) publisher or from a similar extradiegetic position.

To sum up, what I here refer to as voice seems not to be identifiable as a singular speaker but, rather, as a composite, mechanical chorus coming from both inside and outside of the intrigue envelope. To classify this group as a narrator seems to be inappropriate, because the most narrating voice is also the least dynamic one and also because the voices do not fit together as one whole person nor even as several individuals. Instead, they are perhaps an imperfect simulacrum representing the intrigant and speaking with several tongues. Furthermore, the relationship between this chorus and the intrigant does not match that of a narrator and an implied author. There are parallels, but in the adventure game it is the intrigant, rather than the impartial voice positions, who schemes for successful development of the intrigue and who is the opponent of the intriguee. This implied being is not identical to the implied author or programer of the game. As Per Aage Brandt notes, "the user cannot but feel guided by an already instantiated, implemented intentionality" (1993, 133); but Brandt assigns this symbolic entity to the "*designer* of the machine," in other words, to the implied programer and, thus, not to the intrigant as an emergent, immanent position.

To illustrate this difference with a more nearly universal example, consider the imaginary being we invoke when we address our (ill-behaving) computers as "him" or "it" (e.g., "Oh no, he crashed again"). We are not referring to the person who wrote the program we are using (the implied programer) nor to the voice that informs us that things have gone wrong ("Bad sector reading drive A:")—because often there is no such report, just the bad news itself—but to that eternal whoever-it-is who ultimately controls every program we use and who is, quite deliberately, driving us crazy with its irrational behavior. This is the intrigant: an unwelcome devil in real life but a pleasure-giving Mephistopheles in the cybertext.

When it comes to perspective, there seems to be an unclear boundary between the voice and the player's puppet, which indicates that the puppet's subject position (or what Aristotle referred to as *dianoia*, the thoughts of a character) is a contested site in the unfolding of the intrigue. "I'll be your eyes and hands," says the voice in *Adventure* (see Buckles 1985, 141), but sometimes the voice also takes control of the thoughts and will of the puppet, often to the great annoyance of the player, as this example from *Deadline* shows:

PLAYER: Drink scotch.

VOICE: You take a small swig of the golden fluid, which burns as it goes down.

PLAYER: Again.

PLAYER: It's one thing to take a bracer on occasion, but you must resist the temptation to indulge too often.

The intrigue in *Deadline* does not include a drunk puppet, so the player is allowed a small virtual taste, and only once.

Other times, the player's persistence eventually pays off but not the way one expected:

PLAYER: Hit leslie with roses.

VOICE: You rethink your planned action.

PLAYER: Hit leslie with roses.

VOICE: You rethink your planned action.

PLAYER: Hit leslie with roses.

VOICE: With a lethal blow of your hand, Mrs. Robner falls dead. Your mind becomes confused amidst strange screaming, yelling, and the pangs of your conscience. "How could I have done it?" you ask yourself, as you hear the distant sound of police sirens. Sergeant Duffy and two other officers enter and grab you rather unceremoniously. They take you to a waiting car, where, forlorn and disgusted, you begin to ponder prison life. "Perhaps," you think, "I shouldn't have done that."

Here we can observe how, to punish the noncooperative intriguee, the intrigant must break the illusion of free interaction and instate first thought control, then narrative control. This makes it look like the player's fault, for persisting in disobeying, but in reality it is the intrigant who has broken the ergodic contract, as the return to a narrative mode shows. Ironically, noncooperation and free play result in narrative punishment, which equals the end, death. The model intriguee, in other words, is a good puppet, which indicates that the intrigant of *Deadline* is not the autonomous ruler of the simulated world but something of an impostor and a hypocrite, an old-fashioned author dressed up in the latest technology. As Stuart Moulthrop writes about hypertext, "The text gestures toward openness—*what options can you imagine?*—but then it forecloses: some options are available but not others, and someone clearly has done the defining. The author persists, undead presence in the literary machine, the inevitable Hand that turns the time" (1991b, para. 21).

But even (and especially) the most authoritative texts include the means of their own deconstruction, and *Deadline* is no exception. Sometimes, the intrigant can be too clever for its own good. The simulated people that the player encounters in the game are all quite wooden, half-living, and as we saw when we tried to talk to Duffy ("You can't talk to the Duffy!"), sometimes more of an object than a person. "Sergeant Duffy" is actually implemented differently from the other nonplaying characters in *Deadline;* he seems to be without a location of his own but is always hovering quietly in the background, ready to assist. His even more than usually inanimate nature is revealed when we treat him like a normal nonplaying character and try to ask him questions, (which normally results in the reply quoted above). But sometimes the intrigant gets it right without trying, as when we say, "accuse Duffy," and are told, "What a detective! Quick, Sergeant! Arrest that Sergeant Duffy!" This seems to be a lucky coincidence, because exactly the same canned ironic reply is given when we accuse other objects ("Quick, Sergeant! Arrest that saucer!").

Many absurd events result from this kind of mistake (bug) in the intrigue, for example, when you try to sit on chair and are given the reply, "This isn't the kind of thing to sit on!" Examining the obstinate object yields the message, "There's nothing special about the chair"—but indeed there is. And while you may carry the ladder all over the garden, "get the chair" results only in ridicule: "You can't be serious!" Sitting on beds and sofas, on the other hand, works just fine. A more general bug is the nonplaying characters' failure to reflect on what is going on. After one of them has just been killed, Mrs. Rourke, who is "tidying up" in the hallway outside, doesn't know anything about it: "I haven't seen her today."

But if Sergeant Duffy and the other nonplaying characters in

Deadline aren't quite alive, there is one person who is less dead than he's supposed to be. By coincidence I discovered that the clockwork world wasn't running quite on time and that there was a very literal ghost in the machine, as the following log shows.

PLAYER: North.
VOICE: Library.
> Beside the desk is a large collapsible tray. Sitting on the tray is a bowl containing a white powdery substance. Alongside the desk is a wicker wastepaper basket. The wastepaper basket contains: A bunch of crumpled papers. Lying on the floor, overturned, is a beautiful saucer. There is a bottle of Ebullion here.

PLAYER: Question Mr. Robner.
VOICE: Mr. Robner is listening.
PLAYER: Show saucer to Mr. Robner.
VOICE: Mr. Robner lets out a loud yawn.
PLAYER: Accuse Mr. Robner.
VOICE: Robner shrugs off your suggestion.
PLAYER: Kiss Mr. Robner.
VOICE: Section 204D, Paragraph 7.6 of the Connecticut Police Code of Conduct specifically prohibits kissing suspects.
PLAYER: Squeeze marshall.
VOICE: It's unclear how Mr. Robner would take this, so you defer until after hours.
PLAYER: Arrest Mr. Robner.
VOICE: You realize that you don't have enough evidence to convict Mr. Robner, so you resolve to continue the investigation.
PLAYER: Ask Mr. Robner about Mrs. Robner.
VOICE: Mr. Robner isn't here!
PLAYER: Wait for Mr. Robner.
VOICE: That person is already here!
PLAYER: Throw saucer at Mr. Robner.
VOICE: Mr. Robner, puzzled by your unorthodox methods, ducks as the saucer flies by.
PLAYER: Kill Mr. Robner.
VOICE: With a lethal blow of your hand, Mr. Robner falls dead. Your mind becomes confused amidst strange screaming, yelling, and the

> pangs of your conscience. "How could I have done it?" you ask
> yourself, as you hear the distant sound of police sirens. Sergeant
> Duffy and two other officers enter and grab you rather
> unceremoniously. They take you to a waiting car, where, forlorn
> and disgusted, you begin to ponder prison life. "Perhaps," you
> think, "I shouldn't have done that." The case has ended. Would you
> like to start your investigation over from scratch? (Y/N)

This scene is a fine example of the potential for absurd theater
that the adventure game genre has so far not exploited, and it is all
the better for being completely unintentional. Not only is Mr. Robner back from the dead to haunt the scene of his murder, he is also
one of the suspects! (Which makes a bizarre kind of sense, since suicide is one of the working theories.) The final irony, that the policeman ends up as the killer in his own investigation, is a masterpiece
of the cybertextual aesthetics of autonomy and the closest we can
get to a proof that the intrigant is not the same as the implied programer, even when the cybertext is determinate. It also supports my
conclusion in chapter 2, that the possibility of unintentional sign
behavior makes cybernetic media creatively emergent and, therefore, not subsumable by the traditional communication theories.

Intrigue and Discourse

These observations fit well with the rhetoric of hypertext (i.e., the
aporia-epiphany pair) that was developed in the previous chapter. In
the adventure game, a similar master figure of mystery and even-
tual solution is at work. But there are differences between hypertexts and adventure games, the most obvious of which is the nature
of the aporias. In hypertexts, it is always nonlocal, that is, we don't
know exactly what to look for or where to look. In games such as
Adventure, the aporia is local and tangible, usually a concrete, local-
ized puzzle whose solution eludes us. As Buckles (1985, 70) points
out, *Adventure* is episodic, in the sense that the puzzles often have
to be dealt with in order, not in parallel or in a sequence chosen
by the reader and, like the picaresque, have little or no relevance to
each other once they are out of the way. Comparing *Adventure* and
Zork, Brenda Laurel (1986, 76) suggests that "episodic plot structure

seems intrinsic to the adventure game genre," but this is not the case, as the example of *Deadline* demonstrates. Later games, such as *Deadline*, are more dramatic than episodic: in the latter the classical dramatic unities of space and time hold, and the successful sequence of necessary events may to some extent be improvised by the intriguee.

Narrative discourse, even when it is a composite of narrative modes, can always be considered to constitute a single plane or course of communication. If we accept this, then we can describe the difference between ergodic and narrative communication in terms of discourse planes. To make this consideration as general as possible, let us also include the discourse of hypertext fiction in the same model. In a narrative, the discourse consists of the event plane, where the narration of events takes place, and also what I call the progression plane, which is the unfolding of the events as they are received by an implied reader. Here, these two planes are identical, as the reader's progression follows the event line. In an exploratory ergodic text such as hypertext, the progression plane is divorced from the event plane, since the reader must explore actively and nontrivially to make sense of the event plane. In adventure games, the relation between events and progression is defined by a third plane of discourse: a negotiation plane, where the intriguee confronts the intrigue to achieve a desirable unfolding of events. As an example of event plane discourse, here is a scene from *Deadline:* "Living Room. This is a large and impressive room, whose furnishings bespeak the great personal wealth of the Robners. The south side of the room is a large bay window, now closed, which looks out onto the front yard, . . . Mrs. Robner turns to you. 'I don't understand why you missed the will reading. You seem so interested in everything else that goes on around here.' "

The negotiation plane consists of the dialogue between the voice and the player:

PLAYER: Examine.
VOICE: What do you want to examine?
PLAYER: The garden.
VOICE: You can't see that here.

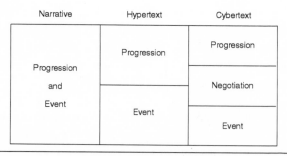

Figure 5.2. Discourse Planes in Narrative, Hypertext, and Cybertext

PLAYER: Go to the garden.
VOICE: You hit your head against the garden as you attempt this feat.
PLAYER: Go into the house.
VOICE: You might try the front door.
PLAYER: Thank you.
VOICE: Whatever do you have to be thankful for?

The progression-plane related discourse is the most formal and consists of commands and questions about the gameplay itself.

PLAYER: Restore [i.e., retrieve a previously saved state of events and continue from there].
VOICE: Ok. . . .

Or:

VOICE: The case has ended. Would you like to start your investigation over from scratch? (Y/N)
PLAYER: Y.

In figure 5.2, this three-leveled structure of adventure game discourse is summed up and compared to the dual structure of hyperfiction and to the single plane of narrative expression. Similarly, the adventure game's intrigue structure is schematized in figure 5.3, with the three levels of the user's position corresponding to the three levels of adventure game discourse. The danger of this model lies in its resemblance to the communication models of narratology,

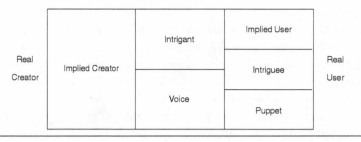

Figure 5.3. Intrigue Communication Structure in an Adventure Game

which may lead to attempts at on-to-one mapping between the two. But as we have seen, the two sets of concepts have such different functions that to use different names is not only convenient but necessary. Unlike the implied author of narratives, the implied creator or programer is not the instigator of a finite train of events but someone who must expect the production of unintentional signifiers, sometimes as unusual as Mr. Robner's strange cameo. The intrigant is neither implied author nor narrator but an immanent adversary who inhabits rather than transcends the game. And the voices, although controlled by the intrigant, are not identical to it, since they appear mechanical and discontinuous yet not without purpose, which makes them also unlike the narrator voices of narrative fiction. The puppet is not a character or a narratee but an empty body, a contested ground zero of both the discourse and the intrigue. And the intriguee, like the intrigant, represents an immanent position but one that must be (re)constructed by the implied user and not by the voice of the event narrator. The implied user, on the other hand, is both responsible for the action and the game's outcome and does not have the implied *reader*'s privileges of tmesis and distancing.

The End of Story?
It is somewhat ironic to suggest that the adventure game is an underrated aesthetic genre that has much to offer and much that is still relevant for the study of textual aesthetics. Not long ago a

young, vigorous, if somewhat bland tradition of textual entertainment, it was quickly overrun by the entertainment market, which preferred a graphical interface for the popular ergodic structures invented by Crowther and Woods. Its revival as a commercial genre seems less than certain at the moment, in spite of some quite interesting and impressive efforts in both academic and Internet-based groups. But whatever its future, and despite the fact that it will never threaten the hegemony of "literary books," as some of its most eschatological commentators have speculated, the textual adventure game should not be ruled out as an interesting topic of study.

In particular, as I have tried to show, the adventure game adds an interesting case to the discussion of narratological concepts and posits an alternative structure of articulating events and existents, one that may help us see these objects more clearly divorced from their usual narrative surroundings than has so far been possible. And—just maybe—such attention will stimulate further research and experiments in the genre, for its own sake, and lead the evolution of ergodic media in another direction than that of the Hollywoodian "interactive entertainment," which can only be the same old escapist nonsense that it ever was but, in this case, all the worse for lack of any decent competition in its own field.

Six

The Cyborg Author:
Problems of Automated Poetics

> The true literature machine will be one that itself feels
> the need to produce disorder. — Italo Calvino

Two main issues in the aesthetics of "literary machines" (to borrow
Ted Nelson's term; Nelson 1987) are discussed here: the question
of human-computer interaction in story generators and the problem of achieving well-formed action in literary adventure games.
These issues are general and theoretical, but I focus on three specific
works: James Meehan's story generator, Tale-spin, the dialogue-
based generator Racter, programed by Thomas Etter and William
Chamberlain, and Brenda Laurel's influential theory of interactive
drama (Laurel 1986, 1991).

These three works — one a text generator developed by artificial
intelligence methods, the second a dialogue program in the tradition of Joseph Weizenbaum's Eliza, the third a theoretical model
of elaborate adventure games — are, in spite of their obvious differences, good illustrations of a fundamental problem in computer
poetics: the aesthetic relation between a human narrator and a machine narrator and what happens when the latter is forced to simulate the former. Using the short story, animal fables, or in Laurel's
case, Aristotelian drama theory, as their generic goal, programers
typically try to get the output of their programs as close to traditional literature as possible, with an ambition to achieve original
prose or "well-formed action" (Laurel). Perhaps more interesting
than speculating on the reason these projects generally (and in Laurel's case, presumably) fail to reach human standards is speculating
on what would result if computer poetics abandoned the "android
mode" and tried to create genres unconstrained by the aesthetic
ideals of narrative literature and Aristotelian drama.

A previous version of this chapter has been published as "Le texte de l'ordinateur est
à moitié construit: Problèmes de poétique automatisée," in *Littérature et informatique: La littérature générée par ordinateur*, edited by Michel Lenoble and Alain
Vuillemin (Arras: Presses de l'Université d'Arras, 1995).

In Woody Allen's 1993 film *Manhattan Murder Mystery*, there is a key scene in which four of the main characters simulate a woman speaking to her lover on the phone. To obtain samples of the woman's voice, they first invite her to a false role rehearsal (she's an actress) and record her saying seemingly innocent sentences. They then edit the recordings to construct the phrases they want and, equipped with four cassette players, call up the target (the film's assumed murderer) to conduct their phony conversation. Even though the process is far from perfect—they play the wrong phrases once or twice and are, consequently, almost dying of laughter—the man does not in the least suspect that he is not speaking with his lover.

Allen's film is a highly perceptive demonstration of the twofold, ironic nature of anthropomorphic machines, what we might call the Eliza effect: the errors produced by such machines can be very funny for the knowing observer; nevertheless, the naive human participants (intriguees) in these "conversations" are capable of projecting sentience, even intelligence, onto their mechanical partners. This aesthetic paradox strikes me as an important clue to the failures and successes of computer "poetics" or computer-generated "literature"—the efforts to create literature with the constructive aid of the computer.

For another example, consider James Meehan's animal fable generator, Tale-spin. Roger Schank offers a very entertaining account of Tale-spin in which he quotes seven of the program's "mis-spun" tales, while not bothering to quote any of the successful ones (Schank 1984). Here is one of the stories: "Henry Squirrel was thirsty. He walked over to the riverbank where his good friend Bill Bird was sitting. Henry slipped and fell in the river. He was unable to call for help. He drowned." (Meehan 1976, 84) In a normal tale, Henry would have been saved by his friend Bill, but Tale-spin was not programed to make Bill act without first being asked to help. Tale-spin was then reprogramed and produced this version: "Henry Squirrel was thirsty. He walked over to the riverbank where his good friend Bill Bird was sitting. Henry slipped and fell in the river. Gravity drowned." In this case, Henry was rescued by Bill, but the agent that had transported him into the river—gravity—was not so lucky, since it couldn't swim and lacked friends that could come to the rescue.

The flaws in Tale-spin's programing produce some quite amusing narrative moments, such as this infinite loop: "Joe Bear was hungry. He asked Irving Bird where some honey was. Irving refused to tell him, so Joe offered to bring him a worm if he'd tell him where some honey was. Irving agreed. But Joe didn't know where any worms were, so he asked Irving, who refused to say. So Joe offered to bring him a worm if he'd tell him where a worm was. Irving agreed. But Joe didn't know where any worms were, so he asked Irving, who refused to say. So Joe offered to bring him a worm if he'd tell him where a worm was . . ." (ibid., 85).

These stories form a striking, if unintentional, parallel to David Porush's concept of cybernetic fiction: narratives that call attention to their "mechanical" structure and "pose as cybernetic devices which ultimately . . . do not work" (Porush 1989, 381; see also Porush 1985). Unlike Porush's examples — texts by Calvino, Vonnegut, Pynchon, and others — Tale-spin, at least in the examples given here, really is a cybernetic fiction device that does not work. And yet it does. The funny thing is, as J. David Bolter notes (1991, 180), that it is Tale-spin's failures, and not its bland and boring successful tales, that are the real successes. They are charming, funny, (unintentionally) ironic; and (the final proof of literary merit) they are the ones that are reproduced, circulated, and remembered. In fact, when reproduced they seem to survive their originator, Meehan: one author (Eco 1994, 110–12) wrongly attributes them to Roger Schank and Peter Childers, while another (Bolter 1991, 179–80) simply refers to "programmers at Yale."[1]

What then, should the politics of computer-generated literature be? I suggest that we abandon the ideal of traditional literature with its established ideas of quality and aesthetics: the computer will never become a good traditional author, if only because it cannot criticize or appreciate its own work. Narcissism is a necessary element in the artistic process, as is self-reflection and self-criticism.

---

1. Paradoxically, Bolter insists that the programer "must share the credit": "The human writer has not been eliminated from the writing process" (180).

The Case of Racter

Concepts like computer-generated literature cry out for clarification. What kind of entity does the writing—the program, the programer, or both together? And in the case of dialogic programs, what about the user? With so many unspecified variables behind the general idea of computer as author, the question, Who or what writes? can only be decided case by case. I propose a typology of author entities, derived from combinations of some of the possible variables involved. Like the term *interactive fiction*, the term *computer generated* is by itself far too unfocused to be useful as a critical concept.

The dialogue program Racter poses a particularly problematic case, since "his" book, *The Policeman's Beard Is Half Constructed* (Chamberlain 1984) includes a much larger repertoire of genres than does the commercial version of the program (e.g., the Macintosh version that I have). The quality of the texts in the book is also on average much higher than that of the program's output. It is therefore reasonable to assume that, contrary to Chamberlain's claim in the introduction to the book, Racter did not "write" it without a substantial amount of help, a suspicion that is confirmed by Jorn Barger's examination of the boilerplate (fill-in-the-blanks) system that allows Racter to form well-constructed sentences. As Barger (1993) points out, the "wacky" style of Racter's output is really Chamberlain's own, the product of a clever human writer posing as a clever program. Not only does the book contain texts produced from far more extensive boilerplates than the commercial, dialogic version is capable of, *The Policeman's Beard* is also obviously compiled by Chamberlain from a careful selection of Racter's gems. Here is a sample from a "normal conversation" with Racter:

ME: Do you like poetry?

RACTER: Yes. Sometimes liking is saying. ha ha . . . HA HA . . . Oh, here's a great one! But, Espen, I cry that poetry affairs are poetry. You speak that I'm insane and poetic, but, Espen, unhinged and insane theoreticians also cry about your expectation or appearance of poetry. Are these your views?

Yet cunning theoreticians will glimpse poetry as a continuing anguish. Therefore theoreticians whispered to other theoreticians "Get set for fascinating stories." Sickening, eh? When a novelist marries a poet, their children are fictionally poetic. Cough. Next question.

ME: What the Hell? [This was not a very fair question, I must admit.]

RACTER: Are all the hells. ha ha ha ha. I'll bet you haven't heard this one: Atheism! Atheism! I'm unhinged and loony and angry! If you drink champagne is that atheism? If you chew meat or cucumber is that atheism? No, atheism is a tragedy and a contract. Champagne is champagne and cucumber is cucumber. Espen, That is an affair!

Damned atheists need Beatrice. Beatrice had many good qualities, like religion, but even Beatrice was afraid of Tasmanian devils. Have you heard this one? A believer physicist crooned "Prepare for a crafty dissertation, Espen." Espen, this is a contract! Next question.

Instead of deconstructing the traditional author-poet, Racter deconstructs the idea of the poet-computer as a randomly driven autonomous compiler of pseudopoetry. In a critical article on Racter, Josef Ernst (1992) characterizes Racter's output as "disinterested" and heavily criticizes the program's failure to engage the reader-user in real communication. He recognizes the closed and "pre-fabricated structure of the program" (452) but fails to recognize the strong human interest behind Racter's highly idiosyncratic style. He dismisses a poem by Racter as something that "looks like a poem and reads like a poem [but] is not a poem" (455), giving this piece from *The Policeman's Beard* as an example:

In a half bright sky
An insect wraps and winds
A chain, a thread, a cable
Around the sphere of water

Strangely, while Ernst rejects the value of *The Policeman's Beard* as literature, he recognizes the qualities of the accompanying drawings that were inspired by it: "It is only [Joan] Hall's illustrations that make the Racter output palatable and printable" (456). Surely, the texts that have inspired valuable illustrations cannot themselves be devoid of value. However, Ernst's dismissal of the poetic value of Racter's pieces, while weakly argued, does pinpoint a real problem of reception: How can art be evaluated if we don't know its genesis? Curiously and perhaps ironically, it is easier to defend *The Policeman's Beard* from Ernst's attack once one realizes Chamberlain's dominant role in its creation.

Far from being the work of a "disinterested" computer program, *The Policeman's Beard* is a product of the symbiosis between Racter and Chamberlain, and so it can be safely assumed that the architect, selector, and editor of the texts is human. The real author of the book is, in other words, a cyborg: part Racter, part Chamberlain. So once again we find a parallel to Porush's concept of cybernetic fiction, in that *The Policeman's Beard* is a product of human activity that merely poses as the product of a machine. Chamberlain's assurance in the introduction that his text is really written by an "other" is, of course, one of the oldest authenticity tricks in the history of fiction and should, for that reason alone, not be taken at face value.

What we call computer literature should more accurately be called cyborg literature, and it is therefore in need of a criticism and terminology with less clear-cut boundaries between human and machine, creative and automatic, interested and disinterested. Cyborg literature, then, can be defined tentatively as literary texts produced by a combination of human and mechanical activities. In presenting a tentative typology of cyborg authors, I hope to encourage an aesthetic theory nuanced enough to deal with cyborg narratives as a separate class of texts rather than as failed pastiches of "human literature."

A Typology of Authors in the Machine-Human Continuum

First, let me stress the partiality and weaknesses of this model: the concept of author entails a certain ideological view of literature, as the last three decades of literary debate have shown. I use the term *author* here only as a label for the positions in a communication system in which the physical text is assembled, without any regard for the social or cognitive forces active in the process. Also, to focus on the author's position necessarily means to marginalize the positions of the text and the reader; a full theory of cyborg textuality would account for all three functions on an equal basis. In a

Table 6.1. Cyborg-Author Combinations

Examples	Preprocessing	Coprocessing	Postprocessing
Scene from *Manhattan* *Murder Mystery*	X	X	
Tale-spin	X		
Schank's version of Tale-spin	X		X
Racter	X	X	
The Policeman's Beard (stories and poems)	X		X
The Policeman's Beard (dialogue)	X	X	X

final analysis, the question of whether any concepts of author, text, and reader are relevant in the study of cyborg literature should be answered. The question of whether any author, in using the techniques and genres of his or her trade, is not already a cyborg is, for reasons of space, not dealt with here.

Given a machine for producing text, there can be three main positions of human-machine collaboration: (1) preprocessing, in which the machine is programed, configured, and loaded by the human; (2) coprocessing, in which the machine and the human produce text in tandem; and (3) postprocessing, in which the human selects some of the machine's effusions and excludes others. These positions often operate together: either 1 and 2; 1 and 3; or 1, 2, and 3; or 1 by itself, although the human operator need not be the same in different positions. Examples: the scene from Allen's film is 1 and 2; Tale-spin is 1 alone (although Schank's description of Tale-spin is 1 and 3); Racter is 1 and 2; while *The Policeman's Beard* is both 1 and 3 (the stories and poems) and 1, 2, and 3 (the dialogues with users). This is summed up in table 6.1.

These very few and heterogeneous examples can obviously not give us any statistically significant results, but the table does suggest some interesting facts that might be looked into more closely in a more extensive survey. As we can see, preprocessing is always present, but coprocessing and postprocessing seem to be almost mutually exclusive. This suggests that systems using coprocessing and systems using postprocessing are found in different contexts and are used for different purposes. However, it is not possible to verify such a hypothesis at this point.

The cyborg author model is obviously very simple, and no attempt is made here to describe the huge range of possible linguistic and rhetorical devices laid down in the machine or computer program nor the possible ways that the input in position 2 can be used (e.g., the difference between Eliza and Racter). This is merely a skeletal outline of three basic elements of cyborg writing, the combinations of which yield four modes of authorship. A future expansion of this model should include rhetorical and linguistic perspectives.

Laurel's Playwright: Seducing the User

In her Ph.D. dissertation (1986) and in her book *Computers as Theatre* (1991), Brenda Laurel envisions an "interactive fantasy system": a type of adventure game more advanced than today's species, in which a central part of the system is a "playwright" who governs the dramatic interaction so as to produce what Laurel, inspired by Aristotle's *Poetics,* calls "organic wholes," with classic dramatic elements such as peripety, catharsis, and so forth. Her ideas have influenced and inspired applied efforts in the field, such as the Simulated Realities Group (the "Oz project") at Carnegie Mellon University as well as individual developers like David Graves (1991).

Laurel calls her envisioned genre interactive drama "a first-person experience within a fantasy world, in which the user may create, enact, and observe a character whose choices and actions affect the course of events just as they might in a play. The structure of the system proposed in the study utilizes a playwriting expert system that enables first-person participation of the user in the development of the story or plot, and orchestrates system-controlled events and characters so as to move the action forward in a dramatically interesting way" (1986, 10–11). Laurel's vision is governed by her use of dramatic theory and by her dramatic perspective on the field; her analyses both suffer and benefit from this. In the definition quoted above, the relevance of the dramatic genre seems arbitrary, as a substitution of the word *play* with *novel* and *dramatically* with *epically* reveal. Her argument hinges on her concept of first-personness: she argues that a dramatic experience is first person, or enacted, while an epic experience is second (or third) person, or narrated. This difference she makes a function of the user interface, in which, in a second-person adventure game, you tell the system what to do and are told in return what has happened (e.g., you: "Feed the troll." SYSTEM: "The troll is not hungry"), whereas in a dramatic "game" you "do" and "see" directly.

There is, however, a conceptual problem here. A dramatic experience, as defined by Aristotle, is intended for an audience and, as such, is just as second person as an epic experience. The position of first-personness, on the contrary, is traditionally related to the lyrical experience, in which the distance between the voice of the poem and the listener is considerably reduced. Using Aristotle, Laurel identifies epic traits in the adventure game *Zork* and dramatic traits in the simulation game *Star Raiders,* but on the whole her categorical liaison is unfortunate. Her conclusion that "Zork is narrated, and not enacted" (78), for instance, suggests that she confuses absence of enacting with what is simply a more abstract level of enacting. The mode of enacting is partly defined by the interface but, in the case of *Zork,* is certainly not prohibited by the interface— although for some it may seem inhibited by it. Whether he types "get thing" or manipulates an icon on the screen, the enactor's strategic investment is the same.

In short, Laurel seems to believe that a work such as *Zork* cannot incorporate both narratological and dramatic devices. Following her logic of interface dependency, a game of computer chess would be classified as dramatic if the user could position the pieces directly with a mouse or a joystick and as epic if the user has to type commands such as "c2-c4." Of course, the difference between a visual and a textual representation or interface is aesthetically important, but it is not identical to the difference between drama and narrative. Perhaps we should recognize drama as a complex subtype of narrative: it is a way to tell a story (drama as interface) as well as a set of narratological conventions (cf. Aristotle's unities of time and action). As we all know, a play can be read privately or it can be played on stage, on television, or on the radio and it would still be a play. Interface, therefore, seems like a secondary distinguishing feature of drama. In introducing the dramatic perspective on ergodic fiction, Laurel has made an important contribution to the field; but it might have been less problematic if she had considered using general narrative theory to counterbalance her use of dramatic theory.

Laurel's elaborate model is an impressive call for a computer simulation of improvised drama, with the user cast in a main role. However, Laurel's insistence upon dramatic control could make her proposal unviable. If the "playwright" is to orchestrate the action into a well-formed whole, of what use is the user? Either users will surrender to the playwright's ideas of acceptable behavior and become docile servants of the narrative, or (more likely) they will revolt against the system's narrative goals and turn the "play" into a subversive metanarrative, with a well-formed ending out of reach.

Laurel's dependence on drama theory cripples the potential of adventure games to develop into a richer art form, one in which the rigid structure of do-the-right-thing-in-the-right-sequence-or-you'll-be-sorry poetics can be replaced with a gentler and freer model in which users employ their creative energies in a world, not in a generative model of a linear genre. Laurel's playwright-in-machina approach disregards the fact that when the user is allowed freedom of action the usual laws of linear expression drama no longer apply.

As Janet Murray (1991, 12) and others argue, the adventure game type of computer textuality is hardly one where the "author" has given up control. Rather, the user can be manipulated in new and powerful ways. In a narrated, linear expression text, the user/reader/receiver's response and interpretation are beyond the control of the author, who can only hope that the text will be read from beginning to end. As we have seen in previous chapters, in a hypertext, the author can make sure that the user must go through a particular sequence to access a certain part; in an adventure game, the author can even make the user perform detailed and distasteful symbolic actions (e.g., "kill the old pawnbroker lady with the axe") in order to continue in the game. As with most games, the rules are well beyond the player's control, and to suggest that the user is able to determine the shape of such a text is the same as to confuse the influence of a city's tourist guide with that of a city planner.

There is little doubt that the "playwright," in terms of user freedom, represents a more flexible regime that the intrigant of traditional adventure games, and that Laurel's system, if built, would represent an interesting contribution to the medium of computer-generated literature. Nevertheless, the choice of a traditional poetics (i.e., Aristotle's), and implicitly, the "well-formed action" of "literary values" is unfortunate, for the following five reasons:

1. As I argue with Tale-spin, the failures of an authoring system seem to be much more interesting than its successes. Today's artificial intelligence techniques are simply not intelligent enough (or should I say, creative enough) to emulate traditional fiction authors or dramatists. So instead of a well-formed, poetically correct result we would at best get an interesting, entertaining failure. This is a critique not so much of the resulting text (which might turn out to be a lot of fun) as of the unrealistic intentions behind it.

2. Human playwrights (Sophocles, Ibsen, Pinter, etc.) do not have to improvise the action on the run; much less do they have to put up with a main character with a will of its own. Laurel's playwright, therefore, has a much harder task than its human colleagues, who can take their time and even change the play after rehearsals with a director and real actors.

3. Who decides the genre? A human author has no trouble mixing genres and changing goals in real time. But could a rule-abiding program do it? Will the playwright be able to cope if the intriguee suddenly changes from Henry the lovesick gallant to Henry the serial killer? And back again? Maybe a genre-switching feature could be programed into the system; but then there goes the organic whole out the window.

4. Who decides the ending? If the action is enjoyable, why quit? If the system is programed to end the "performance" once certain goals are achieved, the user will soon learn to avoid these concluding situations. Again, the assumption that a human player would accept the working conditions of a fictitious character seems more than a little unrealistic.

5. If Laurel's systems poetics is to be successful, it must seduce the user into following the planned action. It cannot use force, for that would only draw attention to the dumb, mechanical entity that are calling the shots, as we saw in *Deadline*. However, seducing the user means playing on his baser instincts (vanity, libido, etc.); this is hardly a way to achieve the Aristotelian ideals.

The main argument for a poetics of Laurel's type is that there must be thematic focus and constraint in a fictional world; artistic quality cannot be reached without inner coherence and creative limits. It would be unfair to dismiss this as merely the wish to recreate an old aesthetics inside a new one or as the easy way out for lazy programers who do not want to simulate too many aspects of reality. Laurel and other proponents of the directed poetics school have thought long and hard about their models, and before they present a running prototype of their system any criticism will remain speculative. Even so, it is legitimate to criticize their premises. The most serious problem is that, caught by the theatrical metaphor, the playwright paradigm treats the implied user on the one hand as a dramatis persona and on the other as an audience; in other words, both as an agent without a will and as a watcher without a say. The real user, however, is neither, and given a fair range of possible actions it will behave like a real person (with the added excitement of an unreal world) and not like a puppet. To paraphrase Laurel's dictum that we should "think of agents [the artificial personae in a game] as characters, not people" (1991, 145), we should regard players as people, not characters.

A game system without a "playwright," like a world without a god, would perhaps appear meaningless to the outside observer. No well-formed action there. But, also like the real world, it would not be without constraints. On the contrary, a game system without a top-down narrative or a dramatic structure would rely solely on the simulation model's qualities for its playability and realism. The intrigant would still be at large, as the personification of what the player is up against when she is trying to beat the system. This system would not be able to camouflage simplistic design with directed interventions from above, as the early adventure games did. It would also realize the obvious, but perhaps in our TV-age half-forgotten, principle about games: the real fun is in participation, not in watching others play.

From Author Simulacrum to Cybertext

There are, as discussed above, two main problems in contemporary computer-generated poetics. One is the use of traditional literary genres and formats as the ideals of the new literature, thus setting up unrealistic (and irrelevant) goals. The other is the uncritical use of traditional literary theory in the criticism of participatory literature, thus hindering an investigation of these new ergodic forms that will emphasize how they differ from narrative media. Unlike the textual aporias of hypertexts and adventure games, the aporias of computer-generated literature can be located in the programers' ideological attachment to narrative ideals. I suspect the epiphany of poetologists of the computer-generated school will come only when they see this as a problem.

To achieve interesting and worthwhile computer-generated literature, it is necessary to dispose of the poetics of narrative literature and to use the computer's potential for combination and world simulation in order to develop new genres that can be valued and used on their own terms. Instead of trying to create a surrogate author, efforts in computer-generated literature should focus on the computer as a literary instrument: a machine for cybertext and ergodic literature. As we have seen in the previous chapters, the computer as literary agent ultimately points beyond narrative and toward ergodic modes—dialogic forms of improvisation and free play between the cyborgs that today's literate computer users (and their programs) have become. What we need in order to achieve this is not an automated playwright or narrator but simulated worlds with emergent intrigants, interesting enough to make real people want to spend time and creative energy there.

Songs from the MUD:
Seven Multiuser Discourse

> We think in generalities, but we live in detail.
> —Alfred North Whitehead

Literature in the MUD?

In this chapter, which examines the last of the subcategories of this study, I try to avoid both the anthropological-psychosocial perspectives and the avant-garde constructivism that multiuser discourse inevitably invites. Almost nothing about multiuser discourse as literary phenomenon has yet been researched, let alone published, which means that my approach here is even more provisional than usual.[1] As a player on the original *TinyMUD* and several other MUDs at that time (1989–90), I draw on personal experience in the following discussion. It feels somewhat strange to situate my knowledge in this way, but given the strongly chronological nature of MUD discourse—in which, unlike the other main texts in this study, the historical moment of the implied user becomes an empirical factor—it should establish my perspective more clearly.

In the earlier chapters, the main texts are clearly identifiable as the work of one individual or of a group of individuals who share a set of goals. Even if the behavior of these texts has been unstable, unpredictable, or even unexpected, they retain some coherence or, at least, systematic disorder and possess the necessary integrity to be identified as works of literature, meant for textual pleasure and produced by someone for someone (else). Even John Cayley's *Book Unbound* (1995a) can be discussed and referred to as a literary work, which indicates that its subversive aesthetics are still subject to the boundaries and laws of a genre that it is trying to, if not escape, then at least negate. At some level in all these works we observe an overarching structure, which may not be intentional, and which may

---

1. For excellent introductions to general aspects of MUDs, see Amy Bruckman (1992) and Elizabeth Reid (1994).

well be a social illusion, but which nevertheless is "there" enough to give the work the sense of wholeness that we need to see it.

As Michel Foucault (1988) argues, the (social) construction of a literary work is less a matter of composition than of authorization. Similarly, next to Foucault's "author function" we may posit a title function whereby texts become (named) documents rather than nameless and boundless printouts, logs, listings, or scribbles, and in this way they become visible and accountable to critics, myself included. All the texts in my study, by presenting a title, project an aura of unity that they might otherwise not command. All, that is, except possibly the most "western" text on the east-west axis of figure 3.2 and, therefore, arguably, the most cybertextual of the cybertexts in this study: *TinyMUD*, also known as *TinyMUD Classic*, the multi-user dungeon that ran from August 1989 to April 1990 and that no longer exists except as an inactive database file.

The acronym for the game *Multi-User Dungeon* is *MUD*. However, social scientists doing research on the MUD phenomena often refer to MUDs disingenuously as multiuser domains, multiuser dialogues, or even, incongruously, multiuser dimensions, to avoid association with the embarrassing term *dungeon*, which might remind their readers (and tenure committees) of the MUD's puerile origin as a game. Surprisingly, no one has yet, to my knowledge, suggested the rather obvious alternative term *discourse.* I do not advocate such a change, however, because the term *dungeon* best retains the special flavor of MUDs compared to other multiuser systems, such as Internet relay chat (IRC), their pseudo-physical spaces, and the adventurers that inhabit them. Elizabeth Reid (1994) notes wryly that "some would insist that MUD has come to stand for Multi Undergraduate Destroyer, in recognition of the number of students who may have failed their classes due to too much time spent MUDding" ("Background Chapter," n. 12). Similarly, the term *MOO* (which stands for MUD, object oriented) is often used synonymously with the term *MUD*, as this is the type of MUD most commonly used by researchers.

How can a multiuser database system such as tinyMUD be a text, let alone literature? The first assumption stretches an already elastic

concept to its outer material limits, which may not be such a problem (see chap. 2), but the latter question, about literature, is not so
easily dismissed. In tinyMUD and other multi-user dungeons, there
are no authors, publishers, or markets, only writers of various types.
What they produce is not meant for literary immortality, and their
nameless or pseudonymous efforts should not be regarded as part of
what Pierre Bourdieu (1986) terms the "accumulation of symbolic
capital," by which he refers to the artist's or cultural worker's legitimate means to get recognition and, ultimately, economic profit by
participating in the field of literature. As Bourdieu explains, "For the
author, the critic, the art dealer, the publisher or the theatre man-
ager, the only legitimate accumulation consists in making a name
for oneself, a known, recognized name, a capital of consecration implying a power to consecrate objects (with a trademark or signature)
or persons (through publication, exhibition, etc.) and therefore to
give value, and to appropriate the profits from this operation" (132).

In a limited sense, MUDs are autonomous systems of symbolic
capital, and the "names" of users can, in a weak way, be regarded as
means of accumulating capital within the field, or power structure,
of the particular MUD, but as an explanation of the motivation for
MUD participation, this analysis breaks down very quickly. The use
of anonymity, multiple nicknames, identity experiments (e.g., gender swapping), and a generally ludic atmosphere suggests that the
participants are not out to strengthen their position in society but
rather to escape (momentarily) from it through the creation of an
ironic mirror society that will allow any symbolic pleasure imaginable.

Admittedly, I am here idealizing the MUD as a utopian, almost
pastoral, free space, in which the burdens and tensions of everyday
life do not exist. This image must be modified somewhat. MUDs
are media for interaction between real persons in real time, and
this means that they can be used for different types of symbolic
exchanges and rituals and are as useful in the propagation of an institutional field as they are in the subversion of one. In recent years,
MUDs have been proposed as nonlocal work spaces for academic
disciplines (see Curtis and Nichols 1993), thus providing a "virtual
department" for an international group of scientists working in the

same academic field. But while such an arrangement may have many advantages, one of the most important is as part of the academic field's social and cognitive infrastructure. Seen this way, MUDs may provide an effective means for the extension of a Bourdieuian field into the digital nonlocality of the global sphere, as do may other closed, nonlocal, social places, such as invitation-only mailing lists and private IRC channels. Internet Relay Chat is a communication system that provides Internet users with text-based, real-time communication channels (Reid 1991).

There is certainly a tendency in recent years toward less openness in MUD communities. In the early days, players would be invited to log on and create their own characters, objects, and landscapes; one reason for this was to make the MUD a more attractive place, with interesting scenery and numerous players. Today the norm seems to be to control player access (and building activity) by having potential players apply formally and by name to the managers of the particular MUD. This reduction of anonymity inevitably dampens the free play of the interaction and reconnects the MUD field with the larger institutional field it specializes in. But there are still "pure" MUD spaces in which interaction is anonymous and disconnected from any institutional demands; and even in the most official and formal of MUDs there is a dimension of play and textual pleasure.

Typical users of informal MUDs have not asked for literary (or any other kind of) recognition, so my investigation of their work may seem an act of appropriation, intrusively construing their activities as something they never intended. It should not be forgotten that the text type we are dealing with is inhabited by real people, in a most direct and nonfictional way. When MUD users argue that MUDs are not games to them but important parts of their lives, we have no reason not to believe them and a strong ethical incentive to take their claim seriously. Indeed, MUDs of the tiny variety are not games, for the simple reason that there are no immanent rules to regulate social and linguistic behavior. Any system that must regulate its discourse by social pressure and convention rather than by clearly defined regulations is more than a game—both more real and more perilous. This is of course true for any kind of contemporary writing, but for these writers the MUD is their primary or only channel of expression, intended for the very small audience of either their fellow players or only themselves, and they do not see their activity as a self-conscious bid for commemoration in society at large, but at most in the microworld of the MUD.

And yet, MUDs are textual phenomena, based entirely on the activity of writing in an aesthetic, typically pleasure-driven mode. This makes them valuable to those interested in the development of new literary aesthetics and to those who want to study the conditions of written communication in the age of computers and telematics. MUDs are in a sense archetypal, as they emulate and combine functions from almost all other writing media in a social setting in which everything is communicated through words. On the other hand, these on-line social spaces are often, possibly because of their provision for role-play, regarded as sad substitutions for "real" life. Even among social researchers who observe and experiment with the MUDs, such text-based social interactions are sometimes referred to as "virtual communities," as if real community cannot take place in digital, nonlocal communication but needs a physical, tangible space to exist properly.

Here as elsewhere, the rhetorical figure of virtuality seems to suggest that MUDs are examples of a Derridean *supplément,* an addition to or expansion of the privileged modes of social interaction but at the same time an inferior substitute, a sinister dark-side consequence of modern technological society. Since MUDs are nothing if not perfectly logical products of the historic evolution of society, a technologically refined answer to the social forces that have produced books, mail, telegraphy, newspapers, telephony, and so on, we might acknowledge their presence with a little more serenity than is currently seen in their reception by the "old" media. MUDs are currently being used for all sorts of purposes, from *Dungeons and Dragons*–style gaming via informal socializing to doctoral dissertation defenses.

However, MUD writing can also easily be construed as avant-garde, as the ultimate escape from the tyranny of the printed letter, from the author function, from the publishing industry, from the decadence of institutionalized art, and so on. In a more informal forum I once suggested that instead of propagating hypertext, to "find 'the new writing' we must look elsewhere . . . towards UseNet, IRC and the MUDs."[2] And while I intended the remark as an ironic commentary on our need to construct an object called "the new writing," I later found out that I had been interpreted as a proponent for the MUD being a more properly subversive literary medium than hypertext. This was not at all an unreasonable interpretation, but it demonstrates how readily co-optable the MUD (and indeed any remarkable or "exotic" technological medium of writing) is by the pro-avant-gardist ideology of literary criticism.

One voice that has spoken out against viewing MUDs as literary is that of MUD and IRC historian Elizabeth Reid (1994, chap. 1, quoted from an unpaginated electronic version):

> It is tempting to draw parallels between MUDs and novels or plays. The results of the pose, say and feeling commands cause interaction between players to resemble these literary forms superficially, and the social dimension of MUDs can be viewed as a multiauthored interactive text. However, despite this possibility, MUD sessions do not truly resemble scripts or books. The language is simply not the same. It is more dynamic and less carefully constructed. Interaction on a MUD is, after all, interactive, synchronous and ephemeral. Although sessions may be recorded using computer programs designed for the purpose, MUD interaction is not designed for an audience uninvolved in it. This interaction is not enacted to be read as an artefact, but to be experienced subjectively. It is not a text but a context. Virtual interaction loses emotional and social meaning when transposed to a computer file and re-read. The pauses, breaks, disjunctions, speed and timing of virtual conversations are lost in such transposition, and such factors are a crucial signifier of meaning and context on MUDs.

However, it is not that simple. Reid's own stimulating work is an excellent implicit refutation of her argument that a MUD interaction "is not a text but a context," because she is certainly reading it as if it were a text. The differences between MUD sessions and novels and plays are trivial but only on a superficial level, since

2. This remark was made in a posting to the discussion list Technoculture on September 23, 1993, and is quoted in Stuart Moulthrop (1994c, 61).

novels can be written as a fictional MUD session and plays have (naturally) been staged in MUD. To suggest that "the language is simply not the same" is to imply that there is one common language of literary works, which is of course not true—and neither is the idea that MUD language is similarly singular. It is true that MUDs tend to develop specialized rhetorics, but these can be studied and compared to other rhetorical genres, even novels, and especially plays.

While she may appear to be saying that it is the verbal aspect that is different, Reid's arguments suggest (correctly) that it is the technical, social, and (especially) temporal conditions surrounding the language that creates and dominates this difference. The argument that text "loses emotional and social meaning" through the loss of contemporaneity is a far more general claim, which again reveals the logocentric suspicion against the written word as carrier of meaning.[3] But in the MUD context, this seems even more out of place than usual, since MUD communication is perhaps the best example of how much "emotional and social meaning" the written word can convey. Reid argues that the temporal dimension of MUD sessions makes a crucial difference, but the special tempo of the MUD (the users' textual hesitations and impulsiveness and the lags and spurts of the text stream caused by the packet switching of the Internet) should be easy to record and replay with a special program. The fact that such a program does not exist suggests that the temporal dimension is not really indispensable in the interpretation of MUD but merely functions as a sign of authenticity for the MUD user. The loss of temporality does of course entail a certain reduction in empirical accuracy for the researcher, but this is infinitesimal compared to what traditional ethnographic recording methods can achieve in the study of local, physical societies, not to mention the problems of interpreting the literary fragments of ancient cultures.

Like the plays of Shakespeare (and in some ways quite unlike them), MUD sessions are texts. They are to be experienced subjectively and can provide meaning without the absolute need for

3. Compare Jacques Derrida's (1976) discussion of the metaphysics of presence and the ideological privileging of spoken over written language, which is, of course, what the curious claims that computer conferencing is a form of oral language is all about.

staging, although it usually helps. They may not be intended "to be read as an artefact" (neither were Shakespeare's plays), but they certainly are intended to be read. This makes them textual, and the unique aspects of MUD communication make MUD relevant and interesting and well worth comparing to other types of text.

A Historical Perspective on MUDs and Nonlocal Communication

As Allucquere Rosanne Stone makes clear in her investigation of "virtual cultures" (1991), the text-based interactions of MUD are anticipated in a long history of written communication, from the first time people realized that the media afforded an opportunity for communality. It is not possible to recapture this evolution here, but the long tradition of mediated social interaction suggests that MUD is not a peripheral phenomenon in the history of communication but can, instead, be read as a condensed paradigm of the types of rhetorical strategies that develop in nonlocal social systems. MUD is not the playground of a mythical literary language but the kind of playground that preconditions the awareness of textual identity in a much more effective way than previous such social technologies (letters, diaries, notes) could be, since the real-time nature of the social interaction puts the individual under a cognitive pressure that those other media typically lack. In this respect, MUD is not very different from other digital network media (E-mail, news groups, IRC, etc.), but as the medium that allows the freest experimentation with fictitiousness and personality, MUD is certainly the most interesting of these media from the perspective of textual aesthetics.

The first MUD was created by two students at the University of Essex, Roy Trubshaw and Richard Bartle (see chap. 1). In the spring of 1979, inspired by *Adventure* and *Dungeons and Dragons*. Trubshaw developed a rudimentary system; Bartle took over the programing in 1980. The game strongly resembled an adventure game, with the major difference being that several players could be together in the same intrigue. It was both socially oriented and play oriented, with an extensive game world in which players could team up and hunt for treasure, kill dragons, and so on. A slow accumulation of points elevated a novice toward the title and privileges

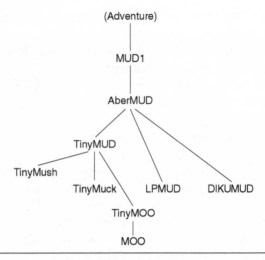

Figure 7.1. The Evolution of MUDs (simplified)

of Wizard, a superplayer endowed with special commands, such as invisibility and toading (rendering obnoxious players immobile). The game became widely known, and players from many parts of the world would log on to the Essex machine at night, when game play was allowed. The game was later commercially available as part of the entertainment offered by large bulletin board systems. It may still exist on CompuServe, under the name *British Legends*, "because CompuServe thought MUD sounded unattractive" (Bartle 1990, 131).

In academia, the first MUD led to a number of imitations and improved versions, at first (as almost always with computer media) programed by students for fun (see figure 7.1). Alan Cox, a player on *MUD1*, developed *AberMUD*, named after Aberystwyth, where it was programed (Bartle 1990, 6). In 1989, James Aspnes, a student at Carnegie Mellon, developed a new type of MUD that almost immediately changed the idea dramatically. Unlike *MUD1*, Aspnes' MUD had no existing objects, intrigues, or world structure but instead let the players build and do whatever they liked. Because of the relatively small size of the initial code and database, he named his MUD *TinyMUD*, but seven months and 132,156 user-defined textual objects later, he had to shut it down because it had reached the memory limit on the machine it ran on. It had become, in Aspnes' words, "a bloated and poorly-managed slum."[4] For some of its players who tried to log on as usual, but who discovered to their shock that they could no longer connect to *TinyMUD*'s machine, it was the end of a world.

Aspnes released the program code of *TinyMUD*, and several people began using it in modified or unmodified form to set up their own MUDs. Other well-known tinyMUDs at that time were *TinyHell*, *Islandia*, and *Chaos* (with its deliberately chaotic topology, *Chaos* was the first modernist, or self-subversive, MUD). Around 1990, a number of improved and extended tinyMUD clones began to appear, with names like *TinyMuck*, *TinyMush*, and *TinyMOO*. *TinyMOO*, designed by Stephen White, was later taken over and extended by researcher Pavel Curtis, whose improved system, *MOO*, has since been the MUD program preferred by academic MUD scholars and media researchers. Also in the late eighties, two other successful, game-oriented MUD games were developed, the Swedish *LPMUD* (named after its developer, Lars Pensjö) and the Danish *DIKUMUD* (named after the Danish academic computer network, DIKU). These two represented a return to the MUD genre's quest-and-monster-oriented origins, but like the original *MUD1*, they could be used for social pleasures as well.

Currently, there are more that thirty different types of MUD on the Internet, and 536 games are listed as running on various machines on the network.[5] In addition, there are probably a substantial number of private and unlisted MUDs, and the genre shows no signs of decline, although the impressive growth in the early nineties seems to have abated somewhat. As for the future of MUDs, it will be interesting to observe whether the inevitable emergence of three-dimensional, graphical, virtual reality MUDs (following the spread of three-dimensional Internet standards such as VRML) will parallel the evolution of single-user games from text to graphics. As

4. Quoted from Aspnes' shutdown announcement, posted to the news group alt.mud on April 29, 1990.
5. This is according to "Doran's MUDlist" of December 9 (see Doran 1995).

Howard Rheingold (1991, 309) predicts, "when goggles and gloves and protocols for transmission of presence make it possible to jump right into a graphic MUD, there will be a population of thousands of sophisticated architects/players."

Because social interaction requires a somewhat more sophisticated channel than spacially oriented, solitary game play, perhaps the textual part of the interface will survive as part of the visual MUD in some form, but as real-time, asynchronous sound transfer (Internet Phone) becomes viable, recorded and live voices could take over many of the functions that text used to have. Or, with the advent of improved voice recognition and text-to-speech systems, perhaps a more complex symbiosis will evolve. Whatever the outcome of this evolution, the MUD will probably continue to incorporate the changes in social communication technologies and will continue to provide an experimental site for emerging social and aesthetic modes of communication.

The Aesthetics of Nonlocal Discourse

MUDs are macrogames and metagames that go on for months, sometimes even for years. Technically, a MUD is a special database server that runs on an Internet machine, usually, but not necessarily, under the Unix operating system. Players connect to this machine from their own machine using a Telnet protocol, typically a standard Telnet program that gives them an 80-by-24-column screen, but specialized MUD clients with user-definable macrofunctions may also be used. Several hundred players can in principle be connected to the same game, but a large number of simultaneous connections slow down response time and depend on the resources available on the server.

In a MUD, the players log on and connect to their own, usually self-defined, puppet and engage in activities that are determined by several factors: the type of MUD, the interests and inclinations of the player, and the interests and inclinations of the other players. If the player is experienced, well known to the other players, and familiar with the MUD, the type of interaction might be very different from that of a new, inexperienced, and incognito player. But they might both just hang out in the central chatting area (often known as the rec room) of the MUD, in which case it might not be obvious from their behavior who is experienced and who is not. Players typically seek out other players (through the location of their puppets) whose company they enjoy, or if they are deprived of this option, they might engage in conversation or role-play with strangers, or alternatively, they might behave obnoxiously, for reasons best known to themselves. Or they might perform all three types of action simultaneously, either through multiple puppets or through the whisper or page functions, which allow communication with players on a one-to-one basis.

If a player is new to the game, he may create a new character with a uniquely identifying name and secure it with his own password, or he might instead take a look around using the dummy character, "guest," if it is available. If he has played there before, he will usually connect with his existing character and take up playing where he left off. Creating a character for oneself is fairly simple and is often explained in the log-on greeting that is displayed when the user connects to the MUD. The command for this is on the form [create username password], so if I want to make a new character—called, say, Godot—I type in "create Godot pass," and a new character arrives in the MUD. I may then proceed to give the Godot character a description by typing something like "@desc me = You see a man worth waiting for. His hair is white, and his hands shake perceptibly as he turns to you and says, 'I got lost on my way to the rec room. I hope I'm not too late.'" (The @ is used as a special system character signifying that a textonic or configurative command is to follow.)

Later, if other users in the same room as Godot become curious as to what he looks like, they may type "look Godot," and the scripton "You see a man . . ." is sent to their screens. Using similar @ commands, users can build new rooms, connect (link) them, create and describe objects, and change their own names, descriptions, and passwords. A very important aspect is the ability to attach descriptions to the actions performed on an object. There are four types of such descriptions, if we disregard the description resulting from the "look" action. For example, if you should see a lamp lying in a room and you try to pick it up, you get one of two possible types of description, depending on whether your action was successful or not.

If you manage to pick it up, you might read "You steal the lamp. Unfortunately, it is just a piece of useless junk./Taken." (If there is no message programed by the lamp's maker, you will just see the scripton "Taken.") Other players with a character in the same room might see a scripton saying "Godot picks up the lamp but realizes it is of little use." If the object is locked in place, however, you might get an error scripton saying "You try to steal the lamp, but it won't budge. Suddenly you hear alarms go off all over the building!" The other players present might get the message "Godot sneaks up on the lamp, but is too clumsy to steal it." This pseudoexample shows some of the MUD's mimetic strength, the ability to create an illusion of complex events with a minimum of simulation and just a few simple descriptions. This device is often used to compromise unsuspecting players, by having them trigger messages that will be seen by everyone but themselves.

The most powerful mimetic device, however, is the *pose*, which is much simpler to use. Simply by typing a colon (:) in front of a verb phrase, any event imaginable can be "imitated" by the users. Thus, if Godot types ":gives everyone in the room a jolly handshake, except you.", then all users in the room will see "Godot gives everyone in the room a jolly handshake, except you." on their screen. Instead of the predefined, finite set of actions in a plot-controlled cyber-text, MUDs allow an infinite set of illusive quasi actions, with no simulated model behind them. This poetic freedom puts the MUD phenomenon closer to the tropes and figures of linear expression literature than many other types of cybertext and establishes it as perhaps the ultimate "literary" game.

The more puppets assembled together in a room, the more confusing it gets, with new scriptons constantly scrolling in on the screen. Here is a short example, recorded in the famous rec room of *TinyMUD Classic* (scripton numbers are mine):

[1] Julia has arrived.
[2] Stinz says, "Julia, may I have some pennies?"
[3] Quist says "EVERYONE KILL JULIA!!!!!!"
[4] Raxas bonks Julia.
[5] Storm has arrived.
[6] Storm waves!

[7] Julia says, "Sorry, Stinz, you're too new. Wait an hour and ask again."

[8] Mooncat rubs against Julia's metal leg in a friendly manner.

[9] Julia says "I'm sorry, Quist, I don't like violence."

[10] Julia says "OIF, Raxas!"

[11] Julia has left.

[12] Skye killed Julia!

[13] Gadget skritches Lynx into a furry, purry puddle.

[14] Storm says "Julia, please give me pennies."

[15] Raxas laughs.

[16] Lynx checks: Mooncat from Quartz?

[17] Storm says, "Gadget, Lynx, hi! Nice to see a familiar face here."

[18] Stinz says, "Heya Storm! *WAVES*"

[19] Sammael says, "A kind of a syntax diagram."

[20] Sammael says, "Form, formula—something like that. I try to avoid it."

[21] Sammael says, "Julia!"

[22] Dirque lies back on ol' lynxie poodle muffkins.

[23] Edsel has arrived.

[24] Storm waves to Stinz.

[25] Julia has arrived.

[26] Skye has left.

[27] Julia killed Skye!

[28] Edsel is off to the Great Hall of Immensity, which is bigger than anything you can concieve of, really because it is so really really really really big and large and huge and giant.

[29] Edsel has left.

[30] Skye has arrived.

[31] Sammael grins.

[32] Raxas laughs at Skye and Julia.

[33] B'Stard says, "Gadget: for example NUMBER = DIGIT { DIGIT|"."}."

[34] Mooncat shakes her head no. Just Luna's temporary character.

[35] Lynx pillows out obligingly for Dirque.

[36] Julia has left.

[37] Skye killed Julia!

There are many parallel actions and dialogues going on here. Julia's arrival in [1] causes [2] and [3], [3] provokes [12], which

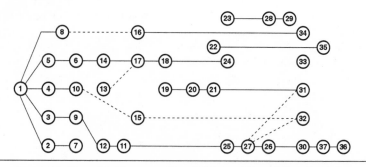

Figure 7.2. Causality Diagram of Parallel Action Threads in a MUD

causes [25], and so on. Figure 7.2 is an approximate causality diagram. As we can see, observed from the outside, life in the MUD can be fairly complicated. And from the user's perspective, in medias res, the action is not much more coherent. Things happen quickly; events hatch, unfold, "intertwingle," and scroll past in seconds. If you do not read it when it appears, it may be too late. It must also be noted that this is only one puppet's perspective of one room in the MUD. A user can have several puppets "awake" simultaneously in one MUD; two puppets at different locations may "page" messages to each other; a user can change the puppet's name at any time; and some users may even play in several MUDs at once — and with the same coplayers.

Interestingly, Julia, by far the most active player (involved in nineteen of the thirty-seven scriptons), was actually a nonplaying character, or 'bot, and was probably the most famous of the *Tiny-MUD* 'bots.[6] 'Bots are external programs logged on just like a player and used for various tasks, such as making virtual money (in *Tiny-MUD*, if you wanted to build or kill something, you needed symbolic money), automatically mapping the MUD's topology, keeping track of puppets, or simply annoying other players. Julia (who was friendly as long as she was not insulted) could be asked, "Have you seen TipTop?" and might reply, "I last saw TipTop in the rec room three hours ago." If asked, she might also give away money or even give directions to a specific room, if she had been there herself.

6. Julia was programed by Michael Mauldin, aka "fuzzy" (Mauldin 1994).

Table 7.1. Discourse Levels in a MUD

Discourse Level	Examples
Construction	@desc me = You see the invisible man.
Progression	connect Godot pass
Negotiation	kill Julia = 100 (i.e., 100 credits says she dies)
Quasi event	Lynx pillows out obligingly for Dirque
Event	Skye killed Julia!

Although clearly not "intelligent," Julia performed useful services for the human players and, as the reactions of other players in the example show, provided a substantial amount of entertainment. It was not unusual for an unsuspecting player to take Julia for human, and engage her in conversation on that premise (Foner 1993). Judging by Julia's example, 'bots and nonplayer agents can be effective autonomous parts of the aesthetic role-play in a cybertext and can provide a valuable supplement to the often more arbitrary company of human players.

Several types of scriptons are involved in a typical MUD discourse. These may be compared to the discourse levels of an adventure game, but the crucial extra dimension of multiplayer interaction bestows a deeper resonance on the linguistic exchange. Also, there is the added level of topological and textonic construction, which is not present in adventure games. Table 7.1 suggests a partitioning of MUD discourse. From an aesthetic perspective, by far the most interesting levels are "Construction" and "Quasi event," as the others contain mostly trivial killings, entrances, and exits. On the construction level, the players design their textual environment and set up rhetorical devices to be triggered as quasi events by the other players. On the quasi event level, players improvise descriptions, actions, and dialogue. Even if "nothing happens" in the simulated world as a result of these scriptons, it may still be wrong to call them quasi events, because the aesthetic communications between players are certainly events in their own right.

Similarly, event-level scriptons may entail a quasi-event-like response, and vice versa. This happens frequently when players try to trick other players, for example by posing ":gives you 100 pennies," thereby simulating an event by way of a quasi event. The discursive dominance of the quasi event level suggests that scriptons on this level express the most significant actions in the MUD, which is the textual play and interplay of the users. Structurally, a MUD session resembles nothing so much as a jazz jam session, in which musicians improvise a rhythmic plateau of chords, riffs, voices, and countervoices. In this perspective, the question of the literariness of MUDs becomes self-evident and locatable: not in grand structural schemes, such as prose narratives, adventure game intrigues, or lyrical visions, but as happenings, whose level of success depends on the competence and performance of the group of players.

Netiquette and Discourse

Unfettered by ergodic restraints such as aporetic topologies and generic intrigues typical of hyperfictions and adventure games, users are free to engage their coplayers in any way they like: a player may decide to alternate between exploratory, metadiscursive, episodic, melodramatic, lyrical, picaresque, erotic, comic, didactic, elegiac, surrealistic, rhapsodic, philosophical, burlesque, or mystic experiences, to name a few. In an open MUD, all modes and genres are available for appropriation, and users with building permits may create the equivalence of hyperfictions or single-user adventure games within the MUD topology, by creating and describing rooms, objects, and links between them. The MUD subsumes these other structures, and it is therefore a metamedium or metagenre in more than one sense, as it can be used to emulate both previous forms of expression (even the codex) and multiple styles and paradigms of writing.

Many MUDs put constraints on their users, usually to avoid information entropy, or to protect their players from noise or harassment, or simply to enforce the theme of the MUD. The rules of a MUD are administered by the local Wizards, who will banish and blacklist any player who does not behave, sometimes by toading (symbolically turning the offender's puppet into a "toad," a dead object). Needless to say, the tolerance level (what we might call the behavior envelope) is not the same for every MUD, and some

MUDs may have been created expressly for the kind of symbolic behavior that might get you banished on other MUDs (Reid 1994, chap. 3). In a word, what guides and controls the player's activity in a MUD is not an intrigue but what I call *netiquette*, the etiquette of the net, a loose set of rules or conventions for proper behavior on mailing lists, news groups, and in E-mail. These are usually formulated by individuals who, with the best of intentions, wish to impose a certain standard of polite behavior on the motley and sometimes unpleasant crowds on the Internet, usually by pretending that these formulated rules reflect the wishes and preferences of a mythical majority of net users.

The idea of a global netiquette is of course an illusion, and this helps us to justify the use of the concept in a slightly different way. Every communicative field comes with its own evolved or evolving rhetoric, a set of tropes and figures that are used by the players in that field. This socially constructed repertoire varies in meaning and applicability, depending on the actual site or position within the field, and this situated rhetoric is what constitutes the actual netiquette of the site. The local netiquette is not a point or position in itself but a contested behavioral envelope of tensions and positions, which may or may not be perceived as such by the inhabitants of the site.

Viewed from a MUD perspective, the question of netiquette can be configured on three levels of conflict: that between different types of MUD (e.g., between the social and the gaming types), that between actual MUDs (e.g., between MUDs constructed for different purposes or by conflicting groups), and finally that between the individual player and the collective within a MUD. On the first level, netiquette is a vague, hypothetical ideal, not really contested but mythologized and often misrepresented by outsiders (e.g., journalists and researchers). Insiders will project a similar, pragmatic attitude (e.g., "in our type of MUD, such and such activities are commonplace, while in MUDs of type x, they perform certain other acts, which do not appeal to us"). This attitude is carried over to the second level, but now it has become an aesthetic issue, and players often have comparative experiences that allow them to judge between actual netiquettes, or styles of interaction. On the final level, the question of netiquette has become politicized, and aesthetic statements become allegorical signs expressing the individual player's cohesion with or opposition to the prevailing netiquette of the MUD.

A simple example is the question of topology: Should MUDs emulate the continuous geography of the real world, where movement is geometrical (going north and then south returns you to the place you started), or is such spatial logic irrelevant in a rhizomatic space, in which links may connect any place to any other? This conflict may be read as an allegorical version of the eternal conflict between order and disorder, law and chaos, and so on. Perhaps the MUD that best embodied the topology conflict was *Islandia,* a tiny-MUD that ran from March 11 to November 30, 1990 (Burka 1995). *Islandia* allowed free building, but it was run by a building committee that inspected and censored new areas according to strict rules before linking them to the "public" space of the MUD topology. In particular, *Islandia* did not have a central rec room (the traditional nexus that all players visit and most link their home areas to, regardless of the geography of the MUD), because this did not conform with the MUD's "realistic" geography paradigm.

Not all players approved of this policy, and some started building and linking to a private rec room, hoping to subvert *Islandia's* "topologically correct" structure by producing a more popular alternative within the same MUD. Other MUDs, such as *Chaos,* with its completely impenetrable topology, might be seen as an ironic comment on this conflict, and the contemporary *BloodMUD* was "created as a parody of *Islandia*" (Burka 1995). Of course, there are many other issues that can be viewed in light of the etiquette perspective, and conflict will emerge whenever there is a heterarchic expression envelope that allows several dissonant voices within the same discursive territory.

MUD players are literary cyborgs; they combine the textons of their stored, long-term designs with extemporized, ephemeral scriptons in a composite phraseology that may be literate and skillful or trite and tasteless, depending on the reader's and writer's preferences and experience. Contrary to Reid's claim, stored parts are, it seems to me, usually carefully constructed, while ad-lib scriptons can express a literary freshness that the less spontaneous textual media cannot hope to match. MUDs are not the poor relatives of more artistic textual media but contain a potential for textual complexity and diversity that is far from mastered, or even conjectured, at the present time. Although the notion of improvisation entails a dangerously unfocused and romantic image of the aesthetic process and its performers and might uncritically glorify the writing and reading processes in the MUD (which are, like all improvisation, really based on a complex sense of conformity and collective responsibility rather than on the genius of the performers), it might make us more sensitive to the aesthetics of the MUD exchanges and, I hope, make us see this phenomenon as a meaningful, intelligible mode of literary communication.

Ruling the Reader:
Eight The Politics of "Interaction"

The Death (and Politics) of the Reader

Behind each of the singularistic concepts of sender, message, and receiver in traditional communication theory there is a complex continuum of positions, or functions. (These are not related to Roman Jakobson's [1960] communicative functions.) When I fire a virtual laser gun in a computer game such as *Space Invader*, where, and what, am "I"? Am I the sender or the receiver? I am certainly part of the medium, so perhaps I am the message. Compare Umberto Eco's statement that "what one usually calls 'message' is rather a text: a network of different messages depending on different codes" (1976, 141). If this definition is applied to a computer game program such as *Space Invader*, it becomes nontrivial to attribute these concepts to specific communicative positions: just as the game becomes a text for the user at the time of playing, so, it can be argued, does the user become a text for the game, since they exchange and react to each other's messages according to a set of codes. The game plays the user just as the user plays the game, and there is no message apart from the play.

This epistemological problem comes into focus every time the known media increase in number and complexity. The step from speech to phonetic writing that took place some six thousand years ago in the Middle East is not merely an expansion of the reach of language in time and space, or a splitting up of language into two different media, or a new mode of graphical expression, but an event that creates an awareness of language as something other than its written or spoken realization. To write is not the same as to speak; listening and reading are different activities, with different positions in the communicative topology. Within these categories there are more differences: listening to a tape recording that you can control (skip parts, repeat others) is more akin to reading than listening to a live lecturer as part of a large audience, and both are fundamentally different from a conversation with another person. Similarly, the production of signifiers that takes place in a lonely writer's den is very different from the activity of a team of copy editors in an advertisement company.

To sustain the notion of reader and author in light of the many different media positions available for the general communicant, we must be able to show that these terms are useful as focusing lenses for a wide variety of positions across the media field. There must be no doubt that the set of different functions is less significant than the overarching activities of "reading" and "writing" and that these two can still be distinguished from each other in some meaningful way. This question is of course deeply political; the perceived gap between consumer (reader) and producer (author) is one of the most profound ideological divides in the social reality of modern Western society. (Even to equate "reader" with "consumer" is a controversial value judgment.) To elevate a consumer group to producerhood is a bold political statement; and in the production and consumption of symbolic artifacts (texts) the boundary between these positions becomes a highly contested ground.

Once the position of the reader has become politicized, we get a meritocratic subclassification of the audience into more or less discerning readers based on their taste for certain genres (cf. analyses by cultural sociologists such as Theodor W. Adorno and Pierre Bourdieu). This already problematic division of high culture versus low culture is traditionally limited to reading/consuming as a noematic activity but becomes doubly problematic when transposed onto cybertextual media, in which the extra functions of user participation are seen as liberating and empowering by some and oppressive and authoritarian by others. To understand this problem fully, we need to examine the way these extra functions work and their relationships with the noematic function or functions. Thus we might be able to provide a structural basis for the political discussion, which is at the moment suffering from (among other things) the unfocused and overgeneralized concepts borrowed from narrative theory. It is already clear that cybertext (like textuality in general) cannot be narrowed down to either a liberating or oppressive position but must cover both sides of the politicocommunicative field. A developed concept of cybertext thus becomes a tool for the study of the politics of communication, and this potential responsibility must be kept in mind as we proceed.

But the politics of the author-reader relationship, ultimately, is not a choice between paper and electronic text, or linear and nonlinear text, or interactive or noninteractive text, or open and closed text but instead is whether the user has the ability to transform the text into something that the instigator of the text could not foresee or plan for. This, of course, depends much more on the user's own motivation than on whatever political structure the text appears to impose. These transformations may occur in any medium and are not governed by the "laws" (technical and social conventions) of that medium but, rather, exploit and subvert such laws for esthetic satisfaction directly connected to this kind of trespassing and subversion. Henry Jenkins (1992) gives a fascinating account of how fans of popular television series such as *Star Trek* appropriate and rewrite the narrative universes, transforming the dominant value systems into their own, often subversive, ones.

To be an "author" (as opposed to a mere "writer") means to have configurative power over not merely content but also over a work's genre and form. That is, to be able not only to control all the "poetic" elements but also to introduce new ones. This is similar but not identical to Michel Foucault's (1988, 206) notion of "founders of discursivity" (by whom he meant such men as Freud and Marx; we would add Foucault, himself). We might also talk about "founders of media" as another extreme position of authorship. Crowther and Woods (the adventure game) and Michael Joyce (the hypertext novel), for example, opened up not only new modes of discourse but also, through their innovations, new media. A good example of medium control is Vikram Seth, who manipulated the sentences on the final page in the Indian edition of his novel *A Suitable Boy* (1993) so that the text ran all the way down to the bottom. His readers would not know they had finished the book until they turned past the last page (see Eriksen 1994, 29). Such materiality of literature is seldom, if ever, acknowledged by literary theory, although it plays an important (if normally invisible, i.e., ideological) role in the processes of reading and writing.[1]

To force the responsibility of authorship onto the reader/user (rather than to locate it in the text or medium) is to acknowledge the struggle for power fundamental to any medium: if the difference between author and reader has vanished or diminished (cf. some of the claims for hypertext), then the real author must be hiding somewhere else. Even if we can no longer use the word *author* in a meaningful way (after all, today's complex media productions are seldom, if ever, run by a single "man behind the curtain"), it would be irresponsible to assume that this position has simply gone away, leaving a vacuum to be filled by the audience. If, on the other hand, it is true, as some hypertext theorists claim, that the author and reader are becoming more and more the same person and that digital technology is responsible, then it ought to be possible to support this claim solely by observable contemporary social phenomena and without the unreliable testimony of the poststructuralists, whose arguments are about written discourse in general and not about certain specific technologies hardly known at their time, with the marginal exception of Jacques Derrida (1976).[2]

And yet, how can we explain phenomena such as nonmoderated discussion lists or groups, where participants are free to argue anything they want? These kinds of fora allow anyone with an Internet access and basic knowledge of E-mail or the widespread topical message distribution system called Usenet to enter or instigate discussions on any topic.

These "decentered," uncensored media are emblematic of the view of digital communication (especially as found on the Internet) as fundamentally democratic, antiauthoritarian, even anarchic. But things are not so simple. Leaving aside the more basic political ques-

1. For several interesting discussions on the broader topic of "materialities of communication," see Hans Gumbrecht and K. Ludwig Pfeiffer (1994).
2. Certainly, this holds for the writings of Roland Barthes (1970) and Michel Foucault (1988). See also the discussion of poststructuralism and hypertext in chapter 4. For a discussion of Derrida's explicit comments on computer technology, see Mark Poster (1990, chap. 4).

tions—such as who gets access in the first place, which groups in society are excluded, the lack of technological infrastructure in the Third World, and so on—and simply looking at the active participants (usually, there is a vast silent majority even in these media), we soon see how the informal hierarchy of networked groups tends to exclude and silence dissonant voices. In a discussion list, this is very simple: an unwanted participant can be removed from the list by the "list owner," who may be giving in to complaints from other participants or might be acting on his or her own account. In a Usenet discussion group, the unwanted participant might get "mail-bombed" (his or her E-mail account is flooded with irrelevant messages, making it impractical to use), or the participant's system operator (the local network administrator) might be asked to recall the offending party's access to the network. If the charges are well enough argued, the "sysop" may well choose to do so, without any need for juridical procedure. Even without any of these methods available, constant and concerted verbal pressure and abuse is a very effective silencer. There are as yet no digital civil rights on networks such as the Internet, only the judgment of the local network owners.

As with any communication technology, digital media might be used and misused in the name of liberation or oppression. The power relationships may not be as simple as they have been in the past, but they are still there. Today, a quarter of a century after the first digital networks and the microprocessor revolution, some preliminary conclusions can be made: even if the digital media allow more intermediate positions for media users, technology in itself has no political program and may be used for oppressive purposes as easily as for liberatory purposes. Telephone and E-mail are two primordial examples: they were developed as media for exchanging interpersonal messages very fast and at minimal cost, but their uses quickly spread beyond the expectations of their inventors. Are these media democratic? This is a complex question, which needs much clarification: What do we mean by democracy, for instance? My preliminary answer is no, they are not democratic in themselves. Network media such as telephone, fax, and E-mail work in a rhizomatic way, against the dominant hierarchy, since they give peer-to-peer access across organizational or social boundaries and are perfect for creating and maintaining hidden alliances (cf. the recent neo-Nazi exploitations of the Internet); and for the very same reasons they cannot be considered inherently democratic. Democracy depends on both hierarchy and rhizome and needs the dynamic interchange between order and chaos to remain healthy. The technology is neither a problem nor a solution in this dynamic situation, but it serves both structure and counterstructure equally well. (Which is not to say that it serves everybody equally well.)

With the dissolution of the reader's role into many different positions of activity, ranging from mere observing to the rearranging and adding of elements, the key political question is this: granted that this range of activities is grounded in technological possibility, can it in itself be said to represent a political range, from the passive (= repressed) to the active (= liberated)? Of course not. The activities of a user of an "interactive" media technology are not necessarily the activities of a social voice that makes itself heard to others. A user of a hypertext novel, for instance, who annotates and relinks his or her copy of the hypertext structure, is not on the same level of discourse as the novel's creator. Even an actor interpreting a dramatic role on the stage or on film is closer than the hypertext reader to the creator's position, sometimes to the extent that we speak of, say, Olivier's Hamlet.

Democracy in Cybermedia

Independent of the technological scale of media positions is the scale of social confrontation or communication, where the medium is the mechanism, not the master, of discourse. A passive reader of a document might be in a much stronger political position than the writer of the same document, for example in the case of wiretaps or police surveillance of prisoners' phone calls or letters. Those who control a medium technically and economically are always in a position superior to those who do not. Control is of course not the same as active use but, rather, the power to stop that use (censorship) if deemed necessary. Consequently, in the examples of user empowerment (E-mail, Usenet, etc.), it is not the technology but the ideological priorities of those who control the medium (or its social context) that permit user freedom. The belief that new (and ever more complex) technologies are in and of themselves democratic is not only false but dangerous. New technology creates new opportunities, but there is no reason to believe that the increased complexity of our technologized lives works toward increased equality for all subjected to the technology.

Since the question of social politics and technology in general is mostly tangential to the main themes of this thesis, I cannot discuss it at length here—see instead Winner (1986), Carey (1988), Poster (1990), Feenberg (1991), Moulthrop (1991b), Johnson-Eilola (1991), and Tuman (1992). I would however like to examine one field briefly; the use of computer technology in education.

Most pedagogical applications of digital information technology in literary or philological studies consist of an arranged collection of texts and the tools to explore them. Pertinent examples here are the *Perseus* project (see Crane and Mylonas 1991) and *The In Memoriam Web* (Lanestedt and Landow 1992). The most common exploration devices are hypertext links in the texts, free text-searching facilities, and graphical overviews (maps, web views) that provide multiple entry points through the image or model that implies the main structural relationships of the material as perceived by the editors. In a discussion of another such system, the "Thoreau prototype," J. Hillis Miller (1992) points out how these systems (when used for teaching literary criticism) "tend to lay down predetermined tracks leading away from the literary text and the activity of reading it toward the explanatory or causal force of context" (40). Thus they may "perpetuate outmoded ideological paradigms of historical or contextual explanation." Despite this critical reservation, Miller is optimistic about the potential of such systems: "The electronic book will be potentially democratic not because of some ideologically motivated decision, but by virtue of its technological nature" (39). Since everything is equally available, the old canonic difference of importance between texts will be broken down.

Perhaps so. But any effort to make texts available free of charge on the Internet (such as Michael Hart's Gutenberg project, which makes classical texts available) is not technologically but ideologically motivated, the work of an idealist rather than of electrons or fiber optics. Dissemination of information is primarily an institutional phenomenon; the technology is secondary. The problem with Miller's operational perspective is indicated by his idea of the library: "Such workstations will differ radically from the library of books side by side on the shelves" (39). But the library is more than books on shelves; it is also an ideology, an ethics of information; and this ethics is radically similar to the ideas and efforts behind free information providers such as the Gutenberg project and other sources on the Internet hypertext system known as the World Wide Web. Through such efforts, the idea of the library is sustained, even as the medium ("the shelf") is superseded. More important, neither the old library nor the new Internet-connected workstation should be seen as inherently procanonical or anticanonical. Both can be used for both purposes, and from the start they have been used for those seemingly opposed activities: preservation (inclusion) and selection (exclusion) of information.

To reach a (tentative) conclusion about the effects of computer media on education, it might help to consider C. A. Bowers' discussion (1988) of Don Ihde's terms *amplification* and *reduction* in relation to educational computing: "The use of technology, in effect, amplifies certain aspects of human experience and reduces others" (32). Bowers observes much optimism in the field, which he ascribes to the easily recognized "selection-amplification characteristics of microcomputers," and perceptively points out that the reductive characteristics of the technology are rather less well acknowledged. What then, does educational (especially literary) computing reduce? This question, however simplifying it may appear, can still be answered: it reduces our possibility to empathize with those who are not using the same technology as we, be they our less well-endowed colleagues or our historical predecessors, the texts' creators or their contemporary readers.

This poses a very practical epistemological problem: it removes us from the historical object we are supposed to study, because a digital version of, say, *Pride and Prejudice* is not identical to the original paper-mediated version. How different it might be will depend on the actual computer system, but since a student or researcher may very well encounter only the digital version (for many obscure but digitally available texts, this is already not unlikely) the reading process might differ substantially, especially of long texts. This may be compared to the differing experiences of traveling a scenic route by car or by bicycle. To claim that the text stays the same is to ignore the material conditions that make the text culturally and aesthetically possible. Of course, this "drift of the signifier" will always take place as the material realities evolve (e.g., from leather-bound edition to paperback, and from scriptorium to easy chair), but the move from a primary medium to a secondary one represents a historical discontinuity (see also Poster 1990, 95). On the other hand, the historical object, as the new historicists would argue, is never within reach anyway, and perhaps an "alienating" technology will serve to make us better aware of this.

The technologies of hypermedia and Internet communication systems provide new media for scholarly or didactic communication, but the political relationship between participants is decided by their personal technical expertise in combination with their influence and prestige. The decision to empower students (the end users of the academic institutions) by letting them partake in discussions on equal footing with influential members of an academic field is ultimately not a technological, but a political, ideological decision, since the technology could just as dispassionately facilitate segregation as integration. As Myron C. Tuman (1992, 133) succinctly argues: "Part of the problem seems to lie in our faith that somehow technology itself, like miraculous new medical equipment for seeing inside the human body, will solve our problems—make us a healthier society—without having to be embodied in institutions of social reform. What we discover again and again, however, is that in the absence of such institutions just the opposite happens—that those in the best position to use the new technology do so for their own narrow interests while society as a whole suffers."

Compare this with George P. Landow's view of the two ways "hypertext blurs the boundary between author and reader" (1992b, 70): "First, by permitting various paths through a group of documents (one can no longer write 'one document or text'), it makes readers, rather than writers, control the materials they read and the order in which they read them. Second, true hypertext, such as the Intermedia system developed at Brown University, permits readers to become authors by adding electronic links between materials created by others and also by creating materials themselves."

Whether one agrees or disagrees with the claim that the multi-cursality of hypertext is enough to transfer control from writer to reader, the crucial issue here is whether technology (any technology) by itself can promote readers to authorship. Clearly, Landow's project at Brown is one of institutional reform, and even if he bestows the role of reformer on the technology—in this case, hypertext—it really belongs to him. If the students at Brown have become authors, as Landow claims, this is induced locally by the idealistic convictions of teachers like Landow and could, in principle, have been achieved by older technologies such as pen and paper. A very similar argument is made by Johndan Johnson-Eilola (1991, 96), who also cautions that "the dominant forces in society and technological development make empowerment through hypertext more difficult than might appear at first glance." Even if hypertext systems such as Intermedia may be a particularly effective means for such a liberatory purpose, it is only through their embodiment in social and curricular reform that they will have any political effect. Landow's educational experiments are interesting moves in that direction, but it remains doubtful that his progressive project should be reduced to a technological effect.

However, the most interesting case in point at present is the fast growing World Wide Web, where anyone with an Internet account, access to a WWW server (a computer system that stores and distributes WWW documents), and sufficient technical knowledge of the system may become a publisher, making documents almost instantly available to the millions of Web users on the Internet. From hypertext links in their documents, these self-publishers may direct users to any other document on the Internet, thus creating a truly rhizomatic alternative to the strict hierarchies of the commercial publishing industry. How can this not be political reform through "technological virtue" rather than through some "ideologically motivated decision"? (see Miller 1992, 226).

First of all, with all the praise being sung about the politically empowering possibilities of the Web, it is easy to forget that it does not in itself create these possibilities. In reality, there are two kinds

of Web users: there are "home owners" and then there is a prole-
tariat, who are read-only consumers without access to the means of
Web production. At the time of writing, telecommunication companies in Norway are offering consumers Internet access without
E-mail accounts or disk space for storing personal files. This creates a class of "silent surfers," cyberspace nomads who can roam the
WWW docuverse without a voice or a place of their own.

Furthermore, the decision to link is ideologically motivated. The
owner of a WWW home page is the hierarch of that site, the topology of which therefore constitutes a local hierarchy to counter-
act the dominating space of the global network. The home page is
an ideological map that displays the preferences, politics, and ambitions of its owner. A link leading away from the site is an intentional ceding of power, an explicit acknowledgment of the value of
heterotopia, the other places or pages on the net that compete for
attention. Linking away is a courteous act of solidarity with an unknown user, performed not because it is technologically feasible but
as a contribution to the network community spirit. Of course, since
a page with many valuable links will be recognized as a powerful nexus in its own right, this recognition will reflect on the page
owner in the form of Bourdieu's "symbolic capital." Thus the World
Wide Web is fast becoming much more than a technology. that is, it
is itself an institution. While a system such as this would certainly
be impossible without the technology, so would the technology be
inconceivable without the ideology (in this case, the ideology of
the Enlightenment, the library, and the value of free information),
simply because no one would then have been there to push the technological evolution in this direction.

Authorship, as always, depends on recognition of authorship;
it is a social category and not a technological one. As Foucault
(1988, 202) claims, "the function of an author is to characterize the
existence, circulation, and operation of certain discourses within a
society." Especially in the case of the Web, it remains to be seen
what kind of status will be given to personal publishers and their
documents. If the users of a Usenet discussion group or a hypertextual classroom are to be regarded as authors (and it is not a priori
obvious that they should be), this will mean an institutional change

in the way traditional institutions regard these forms of discourse as well as of how they regard authors and readers. Most likely (this is of course, at this point, pure hypothesis), traditional institutions like universities will endorse *some* uses of media such as the WWW (i.e., those discourses that can be controlled, like electronic journals with editorial boards and official affiliations), while ignoring others (such as personal publishing), in some ways not unlike today's ambivalent, less-than-trusting relationship between universities and popular mass media.

It seems somewhat self-contradictory to claim, as Landow does, that hypertext blurs the distinction between reader and author while at the same time permitting the former to become the latter. Neologisms such as *wreader* (for writer-reader) suggest that this blurring could be merely a question of terminology, but it could also mean that the separation of author and reader is valuable — that we might profit analytically from keeping the institutional and the performative aspects apart, at least until we can study the latter more rigorously. In the next section, rather than trying to identify the new author and reader and constructing a political significance for them, I try to locate the various performative positions and to describe their relations as parts of a creative, receptive sign system, or discourse.

Levels of Usership

Since most of the texts and textual practices discussed in this study differ much from "normal" texts and from each other, especially in terms of their operational use, I dispense with the figure of the reader and instead bring in the user, a much less predisposed character, at least in literary theory. This change allows me to keep the idea of readers and reading connected to its usual meanings, while letting the idea of the user denote all those textual practices that can be observed or imagined, including reading and writing. The user is allowed a wider range of behavior and roles across the field of media, from the observing member of a theater audience to the subcreator of a game world. This distinction is both practical and ideological; it keeps the established terms free from conceptual distortion, and it signals that to apply the term *reader* to a different kind of media practice is an act of appropriation that should at the very least be discussed in advance. Finally, the political connotations of the word *user* are conveniently ambivalent, suggesting both active participation and dependency, a figure under the influence of some kind of pleasure-giving system.

To illustrate the diversity (rather than convergence) of the reader and author positions, let us consider the authoring system called Hypercard; it was developed by Bill Atkinson in 1987, runs under the Macintosh operating system, and was written in the computer language C. An authoring system such as Hypercard is a metaprogram, a construction kit for building other programs, such as pedagogical software. The strength of metaprograms is that they take away most of the pain involved in programing an application from scratch; their weakness that they limit the programer by presenting a predefined range of operations that the programer must use. (For instance, programers must use Hypercard's routines for drawing rather than creating their own.) This may be compared to premodern modes of authorship, in which an author could use predefined paradigms to produce a genre text, without much creative effort.

In these media situations, the developer is also a user but not of the same product or at the same product level. For the developers of Hypercard, I am a user. However, if I use Hypercard to write an application, I too am a developer—but on a lower level. If that application were a system for constructing, say, language training lessons, my users would also be developers—on yet a lower level. And so on. The end users (the users of my users' language training lessons) might also be differentiated by their ability to change or subvert the software. If, on the other hand, I had access to Hypercard's source code in C, I could reprogram Hypercard and become a developer on the highest level. And so we have both user strata and developer strata, overlapping each other but still in a hierarchical relationship (see table 8.1).

As can be seen, here we have at least four different positions on the author-reader scale, as opposed to the usual two in a text with a flat expression plane. Hypermedia such as Hypercard are more, not less, hierarchical than most paper-based media, but a clever user can easily move up and down the hierarchy. The positions are not

Table 8.1. User Levels in a Development System

User Level	Item Developed	Item Used
1	Hypercard	C compiler
2	Lesson construction kit	Hypercard
3	Language lesson	Lesson construction kit
4	–	Language lesson

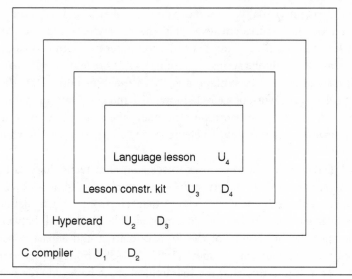

Figure 8.1. User (U) and Developer (D) Positions

personal, since a person on level one might also be found on level four but, at the same time, not necessarily on the middle levels (see figure 8.1). The end user in figure 8.1 (U4) is in a very different position from the developer of Hypercard (D2). This difference is brought on not by the technology but by the user's technological competence and knowledge in combination with the user's institutional position. On a moderated E-mail discussion list, for instance, the weight would be on the institutional position of the user, since all users would have the necessary technological competence (to send and receive E-mail).

This tiered diagram also challenges our notion of text, especially as contrasted to the idea of a system that accommodates certain means and elements of expression. Such a system, S, allows the development of a subsystem S', with reduced expression potential, which in turn can be used to develop a yet more reduced system S'', and so on. But what level equals the "text"? Clearly, the text is a vertical structure; it is expressed on the lowest S level but is equally dependent on the elements of the higher levels. This dependency is of course pragmatic rather than absolute, since the lowest level could remain virtually the same even if a higher level is replaced by a functionally equivalent level or if the hierarchy is reduced (collapsed) by n levels. In other words, a computer program text can be seen as the result of a series of system (S) transformations (T), paradigmatically ($S{\rightarrow}S'$), syntagmatically ($S'{\leftrightarrow}T'$), or both. Thus they are seldom the work of a single individual and are often comparable to a rule-based, premodern poetics, where the poet creates within a framework of clearly defined elements and constraints laid down by others.

J. David Bolter, who chooses to see computer technology as the catalyst whereby the old structures and rituals of reading and writing are replaced by new ones, claims that "electronic writing defines a new level of creativity, indeed a myriad of levels that fall between the apparent originality of the Romantic artist and apparent passivity of the traditional reader" (1991, 158–59). Bolter is certainly correct in suggesting that the hierarchical space between creativity and passivity can be multilayered, but it is hard not to suspect him of writing against his better judgment when he claims that this situation is new, instigated by our latest technology. Why would he call the originality of Romantic artist and the passivity of the traditional reader "apparent" if not to indicate that they are really already part of a more nuanced system of symbolic production? I argue (using Hypercard as an example) that digital systems can provide several levels of creative intervention but that this feature is not limited to electronic texts, nor is it true for all of them (see chap. 3). Electronic writing can just as easily (probably even more easily) maintain the two-leveled hierarchy of a flat expression plane, whereas preelectronic writing (e.g., Queneau's *Poèmes*, 1961) subverts it.

Indeed, the ur-example of such a transformational metasystem is the *I Ching*, which evolved from the trigrams and hexagrams developed, according to legend, by Fu Hsi. These were said to have been recorded on bones and tortoise shells and, later, inscribed on bamboo strips. Around 1100 B.C., King Wen and his son the Duke of Chou added explanations, and around the sixth century B.C., Confucius wrote his commentaries (Sherrill and Chu 1989, 3–8). However, Rudolph Ritsema and Stephen Karcher (1994) claim that this traditional version of the *I Ching*'s origin is a myth "popularized in the Han Dynasty" and that the oldest part of the book is "words, not diagrams and systems . . . assembled between 1000 and 750 B.C.E." (12). Like the origin of *Adventure*, the origin of the *I Ching*'s is not easy to establish. Even today, the *I Ching* continues to be transformed, specialized, and extended (note such titles as "I Ching for the Successful Businessman"). These numerous paradigmatic and syntagmatic transformations and translations of the *Book of Changes* are not to be regarded as perversions or mutations of the text, since in the case of the *I Ching* it seems doubtful that any specific and original text ever existed. Rather, we should consider the "text" as an unfinished historical process of system transformation, the sum of all evolutionary stages and paraphrases.

> Service is more enjoyable when thought of less like a
> story—linear, continuous, temporal—and more like a
> playing field—many-dimensional, discontinuous, and
> spatial.—Edward W. Said

Anamorphosis versus Metamorphosis

ARTIST: It's a tiger. Can you see it?

REPORTER: A tiger? To me it looks like some kind of labyrinth.

ARTIST: It's a tiger, with the contours drawn over and over.

REPORTER: Yes, now I see it. It's a tiger!

ARTIST: Right. The point is to make the audience become a cocreator of
the artistic work.

This conversation, from an art program on the Norwegian radio
channel P2, November 21, 1995, illustrates perfectly what I here
call the ideology of influence: the aesthetic view that (some) works
of art are collective productions, sites of interaction in which the
artist and the beholder come together as equal partners in a creative team and compose something that was not there before. This
creation myth, like many other myths, has some truth to it; certainly a beholder is needed to "make sense" of the work of art. And
not just any beholder; successful readings of difficult works demand
a skilled and trained interpreter, from Umberto Eco's model reader
(Eco 1979) to the *chün tzu* of the *I Ching*. But the problem with this
ideology lies in the fact that the function of the beholder and the
function of the creator are quite separate, temporally, materially,
intellectually, and socially. There is no audience active in the artist's
studio when the tiger is drawn, and there is no immortality for the
successful beholder. All this is obvious. So in what way could the
myth be true? In what sense did the reporter cocreate the tiger?

It certainly did not happen without the artist's guidance. By telling the reporter what to look for, the artist provided her with a
motive for the interpretation, a significant structure on which to

bind the experience. For the ideology, of course, the act of symbolic discovery is meant to happen not this way but naturally, without direction or clues from a previous mapping. Cocreation implies original creativity, some real, rather than illusory, influence. But without coaxing, without a previous reading, as we saw in our discussions of both *Afternoon* and *Deadline*, it is more likely that the beholder gives up and disengages herself from the labyrinth, clueless. The alternative seems too much work, too much trouble. But there are exceptions, and gradually an enigmatic work of art may become less opaque and less of a threat to our thwarted need for mastery. A rhythm, perhaps a sense of order, coherence, begins to emerge. These are the classical ingredients of the hermeneutic processing of a successful work of art. The successful ergodic work of art maintains tension and excitement while providing a path for discovery, a coming into focus of a didactic of the design and hidden principles at work in the work. In some cases, typically adventure games, this coming into focus is in itself a design principle, a necessary part of the user's experience. In other cases, such as an abstract painting (e.g., works by Jackson Pollock), it is optional but enriching. In others again, such as Michael Joyce's *Afternoon*, it may be imaginary but still a necessary illusion for the reader's construction of narrative.

So what exactly is the difference between the ergodic and the nonergodic work of art? If we are to define this difference as a dichotomy (and such a definition may well end up serving the ideology it is trying to unmask), it would have to be located within the work rather than within the user. The ergodic work of art is one that in a material sense includes the rules for its own use, a work that has certain requirements built in that automatically distinguishes between successful and unsuccessful users. The usefulness of this definition is limited not so much by the concept of ergodics as by the concept of the work of art, which, in the case of ergodic phenomena such as MUDs, becomes notoriously unclear.

On the extreme end of the ergodic scale are works that do not make any sense unless approached in a specific way. An intricate adventure game such as *Deadline* can be enjoyed even if no real progress is made and even if the user sooner or later turns away in frustration: even if the communication experience ultimately is un-

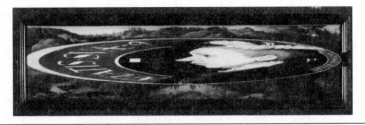

Figure 9.1. William Scrots' *Edward VI*, 1546 (by courtesy of the National Portrait Gallery, London)

fulfilling, some communication has taken place. But there are works that put their users in an either-or mode; either you see it or you don't. The prime example of this is the hidden, three-dimensional image—a plain picture composed of seemingly meaningless graphic "noise" that becomes three-dimensional and meaningful if you hit upon the correct way of looking at it. The revelation is sudden; but it is often not reached at all, in which case the viewer is left with no clue as to what he was looking for. This process is certainly ergodic, in that it requires hard work in the form of concentration as well as conscious instead of automatic adjustment of eye focus and distance, something we have not been trained to do. There is also a certain leap of faith involved, and once one picture is mastered, the next one is not as hard, since a strategy has been learned and, not least, we now can believe that it is possible to extract order from the pure chaos of any other perspective.

But are we the cocreators of these images? Only in a noematic sense. The coded images are objectively there, just like encrypted messages that can be deciphered only with a certain key, and we can no more influence their appearance than we can influence a Rembrandt or a Van Gogh. What we have gained is a perspective, a mode of perception. Although modern computer techniques are instrumental in creating this type of effect, the principle, *anamorphosis* (from the Greek "to re-form"), is much older. In fact, the first anamorphic drawings can be found in Leonardo Da Vinci's notebooks. Figure 9.1 is a 1546 anamorphic painting of Edward VI by William Scrots. The "proper" portrait can be seen from the right (but not from the left!), through a gap in the frame, revealing the visage and the exergue letters in their "normal" shape.

The principle of anamorphosis, then, is to hide a vital aspect of the artwork from the viewer, an aspect that may be discovered only by the difficult adoption of a nonstandard perspective. Anamorphosis is therefore a useful parallel to our concepts of ergodic literature and its master tropes, aporia and epiphany. Furthermore, it allows us an alternative way to distinguish between narrative and ergodic mysteries, for instance between a detective novel of the whodunit type and its adventure game equivalent, such as *Deadline.* For the reader of the detective novel, the narrative experience is not anamorphic, because the mystery is revealed in the standard course of the reading. Even if the reader engages in the activity of trying to solve the case, this in no way influences the outcome of the novel. On the other hand, for the player of a detective adventure game the anamorphic dilemma dominates the experience completely, as the player tries to change the work from one state (unsolved) to another (solved). There is a clear, perceptible distinction between these two states, and typically, once the mystery is resolved, the work loses its enigmatic aura, and usually the player's interest along with it.

Not all ergodic works are anamorphic. (If they were, the concept would be redundant.) Nor does the difference between anamorphic and narrative mystery match the difference between unicursal and multicursal labyrinths (see chap. 1). A multicursal literary mystery such as *Afternoon,* for instance, is not anamorphic, since there is no clear, final state of resolution (or ending) in which all is revealed. Rather, anamorphosis equals the category of determinate cybertext (the northwestern quadrant of the plots in figure 3.2) but not the indeterminate cybertext (the southwestern quadrant), in which there is no such thing as a final state of the artwork.

This last category might more accurately be termed *metamorphic,* as the indeterminate cybertexts transform themselves endlessly with no final (and repeatable) state to be reached. From this perspective we then derive three categories: novels (in which we include *Afternoon*-type hyperfictions), anamorphic literature (solvable enigmas), and metamorphic literature (the texts of change and unpredictability). The tigers that can be observed in the latter are unplanned, unbound, and untamed. But strangely, in these labyrinths our influence as literary agents is much more real than in the two previous ones. Perhaps, therefore, they are also the ones hardest to map with current literary theory.

Toward Theories of Ergodic Literature

I have not suffixed this text with a standard self-paraphrasing summary because I want the various chapters to speak (and conclude) for themselves. To repeat and synthesize their points in a concluding, organic summary seems to impose a finality on them that I do not believe they have. Their goals, if they may be generalized at all, have been to get out from underneath a position even more than to reach one. This dystopia is of course the omnipresent influence of narrative, both as hegemonic theories of discourse and as a socially dominating aesthetic mode. At the same time, like any revolutionary bricoleur, I employ the tools and weapons of the tyrant, with the usual risks of backfiring and of ending up as a mirror image of the previous regime.

As for the new terms, concepts, and models that I introduce, I can only hope they are useful enough to be rejected audibly (and offer some resistance in the process), rather than silently. Any value they may have is probably going to be transitional and will recede as the discourse on (and of) "electronic writing" continues to establish itself among the various "area studies" of cultural critical theory. My extensive construction and use of neologisms, such as *cybertext*, *ergodic*, and *intriguee* is a sure sign of the tentative, rapidly changing phase we are going through at the moment. The idea of the new is always ambiguous, and if the use of these neologisms seems contradictory and self-defeating in a study that seeks to demonstrate the ideological forces behind similar neologisms (interactive fiction, hypertext, etc.), my only defense is that I try to make my concepts less dichotomic and more analytic than their alternatives. My ambition is to make them both readable and writeable (and in a way that indicates the problem with these Barthesian terms, or at least with my understanding of them): readable, in the sense that their denotation should be as clear as possible (admittedly, I am, or try to be, one of what Gayatri C. Spivak recently called the "clarity-fetishists"); and writeable, in the sense that I want you, the reader, to be a user in a transcending, cocreative, author mode. Please use these terms in any way you find pleasurable, please rewrite them, refute them, or erase them, if you want. (Or ignore them, if you must.) Only remember, as I have tried to do, Donna Haraway's recommendation (1991, 150) "for *pleasure* in the confusion of boundaries, and for *responsibility* in their construction."

Many new approaches seem to be emerging in these theoretical fields at the moment and even more in the fields of literary practice. I do not pretend that I have done justice to all (or even most) of them here. When I first started this project, in 1989, I thought I had made a clever choice, because there seemed to be so little reading to catch up on. This is no longer true, and indeed it never was. Except for the field of multi-user dungeons, where theorists focus on technical and social aspects (with a few philosophical, linguistic, and psychological exceptions), these textual fields came with their own canon, poetics, and critical discourse. (In the MUD, however, this meta-discourse is internalized in a way unique and unmatched by other textual forms.) As far as possible, I try to respect these traditions, knowing that the ideological part of my motivation (the other part being curiosity) would inevitably try to rewrite these texts to make them fit my model. I think this appropriation is explicit enough to justify its means, but I welcome any evidence of undue imperialism.

In my constructive approach to the field of ergodic literatures, I feel it necessary to focus on broad, highly visible issues, such as the conflicts between the desires of users and the ambitions of creators or the problems of old terminology and theory when brought to bear on new objects. These are grateful perspectives to engage in, and although they are necessary in an initial phase, their durability is correspondingly brief and must be followed by subtler, less-dilated approaches. I hope I have added a little to the increasing awareness of these literatures and strengthened the argument for their growing relevance to the broader fields of aesthetics and communication.

References

Aarseth, Espen. 1994. "Nonlinearity and Literary Theory." In *Hyper/Text/ Theory*, edited by George P. Landow, 51–86. Baltimore: Johns Hopkins University Press.

———. 1995. "Dataspillets diskurs—mellom folkediktning og kulturindustri." In *Perifraser*, edited by the Department of Comparative Literature, 315–42. Bergen: University of Bergen.

Abrams, M. H. 1981. *A Glossary of Literary Terms*. 4th ed. New York: Holt, Rinehart, and Winston.

Andersen, Peter Bøgh. 1990. *A Theory of Computer Semiotics: Semiotic Approaches to Construction and Assessment of Computer Systems*. Cambridge: Cambridge University Press.

———. 1992. "Interaktive værker. En katastrofeteoretisk tilgang." *Almen Semiotik* 5 (Aarhus Universitetsforlag): 89–112.

Andersen, Peter Bøgh, Berit Holmquist, and Jens F. Jensen, eds. 1993. *The Computer as Medium*. Cambridge: Cambridge University Press.

Apollinaire, Guillaume. 1966. *Calligrammes: Poèmes de la paix et de la guerre (1913-1916)*. Paris: Gallimard.

Apollon, Daniel. 1990. "Dataanalytiske metoder i filologien." In *Den filologiske vitenskap*, edited by Odd Einar Haugen and Einar Thomassen, 181–208. Oslo: Solum.

Aspnes, James. 1989. *TinyMUD*. A multi-user dungeon that ran on a Unix machine at Carnegie Mellon University from August 1989 to April 1990.

Barger, Jorn. 1993. " 'The Policeman's Beard' Was Largely Prefab!" *Journal of Computer Game Design* (August). Also available on the Internet. http://www.mcs.net/~jorn/html/ai/racterfaq.html

Barthes, Roland. 1970. *S/Z*. Paris: Seuil.

———. 1975. *The Pleasure of the Text*. Translated by Richard Miller. New York: Noonday.

———. 1977. "Introduction to the Structural Analysis of Narratives." In *Image—Music—Text*. London: Fontana.

Bartle, Richard. 1984. "Mud, Mud, Glorious Mud." *Micro Adventurer*, September, 22–25. First in a series of seven articles.

———. 1990. *Interactive Multi-User Computer Games*. Colchester, U.K.: MUSE.

Bartle, Richard, and Roy Trubshaw. 1980. *MUD*. Also known as *MUD1*. Developed at the University of Essex.

Benjamin, Walter. 1992. "The Work of Art in the Age of Mechanical Reproduction." In *Illuminations*. London: Fontana.

Bernstein, Mark. 1991. "The Navigation Problem Reconsidered." In *Hyper-*

text/Hypermedia Handbook, edited by Emily Berk and Joseph Devlin, 285–97. New York: McGraw-Hill.

Blank, Marc. 1982. *Deadline.* Cambridge: Infocom. Also published as part of *The Lost Treasures of Infocom.* Los Angeles: Activision, 1991.

Bolter, J. David. 1991. *Writing Space: The Computer, Hypertext, and the History of Writing.* Hillsdale, N.J.: Erlbaum.

──────. 1992. "Literature in the Electronic Writing Space." In *Literacy Online: The Promise (and Peril) of Reading and Writing with Computers,* edited by Myron C. Tuman, 19–42. Pittsburgh: University of Pittsburgh Press.

Bolter, J. David, and Michael Joyce. 1987. "Hypertext and Creative Writing." In *Hypertext '87: Proceedings,* 41–50. New York: Association for Computing Machinery.

Bordewijk, J. L., and B. van Kaam. 1986. "Towards a New Classification of Tele-Information Services." *Intermedia* 14:16–21.

Borges, Jorge Luis. 1974 (1962). *Fictions.* London: Calder and Boyars.

Bourdieu, Pierre. 1986. "The Production of Belief: Contribution to an Economy of Symbolic Goods." In *Media, Culture, and Society: A Critical Reader,* edited by Richard Collins et al., 131–63. London: Sage.

Bowers, C. A. 1988. *The Cultural Dimensions of Educational Computing: Understanding the Non-Neutrality of Technology.* New York: Teachers College Press.

Brand, Stewart. 1988. *The Media Lab: Inventing the Future at M.I.T.* Harmondsworth: Penguin.

Brandt, Per Aage. 1993. "Meaning and the Machine: Toward a Semiotics of Interaction." In *The Computer as Medium,* edited by Peter Bøgh Andersen, Berit Holmquist, and Jens F. Jensen, 128–40. Cambridge: Cambridge University Press.Andersen.

Bruckman, Amy. 1992. "Identity Workshop: Emergent Social and Psychological Phenomena in Text-Based Virtual Reality." Available on the Internet. ftp://ftp.media.mit.edu/pub/asb/papers/*identity-workshop.rtf*

Buckles, Mary Ann. 1985. "Interactive Fiction: The Storygame 'Adventure.'" Ph.D. diss., University of California at San Diego.

──────. 1987. "Interactive Fiction as Literature: Adventure Games Have a Literary Lineage." *Byte,* May, 135–42.

Burka, Lauren P. 1995. "The MUD Timeline." Available on the Internet. http://www.apocalypse.org/pub/u/lpb/muddex/mudline.html

Burks, Arthur W. 1986. *Robots and Free Minds.* Ann Arbor: College of Literature, Science, and the Arts, University of Michigan.

Calvino, Italo. 1993 (1979). *If on a Winter's Night a Traveler . . .* New York: Knopf.

──────. 1987 (1967). "Cybernetics and Ghosts." In *The Literature Machine.* London: Picador.

Carey, James W. 1988. *Communication as Culture: Essays on Media and Society*. Boston: Unwin Hyman.

Cayley, John. 1995a. *Book Unbound*. London: Wellsweep.

———. 1995b. "Beyond Codexspace: Potentialities of Literary Cybertext." *Visible Language* 30:164–83.

Chamberlain, William. 1984. *The Policeman's Beard Is Half Constructed: Computer Prose and Poetry by Racter*. New York: Warner.

Chatman, Seymour. 1978. *Story and Discourse: Narrative Structure in Fiction and Film*. Ithaca: Cornell University Press.

Clynes, Manfred, and Nathan S. Kline. 1960. "Cyborgs and Space." *Astronautics*, September, 26–7, 74–5.

Cortázar, Julio. 1966. *Hopscotch* (Rayuela). Translated by Gregory Rabassa. New York: Pantheon.

Crane, Gregory, and Elli Mylonas. 1991. "Ancient Materials, Modern Media: Shaping the Study of Classics with Hypermedia." In *Hypermedia and Literary Studies*, edited by Paul Delany and George P. Landow, 205–20. Cambridge: MIT Press.

Crowther, William, and Don Woods. 1976. *Adventure*. Available for many computer platforms.

Curtis, Pavel, and David A. Nichols. 1993. "MUDs Grow Up: Social Virtual Reality in the Real World." Xerox PARC. Available on the Internet. ftp://parcftp.xerox.com/pub/moo/mudsgrowup.txt

Deleuze, Gilles, and Félix Guattari. 1987. *A Thousand Plateaus*. Vol. 2 of *Capitalism and Schizophrenia*. London: Athlone.

Derrida, Jacques. 1976 (1967). *Of Grammatology*. Translated by Gayatri Chakravorty Spivak. Baltimore: Johns Hopkins University Press.

Doob, Penelope Reed. 1990. *The Idea of the Labyrinth from Classical Antiquity through the Middle Ages*. Ithaca: Cornell University Press.

Doran. 1995. "Doran's MUDlist." Available on the Internet. http://shsibm.shh.fi/mud/mudlist.html

Douglas, J. Yellowlees. 1991. "Understanding the Act of Reading: The WOE Beginner's Guide to Dissection." *Writing on the Edge* 2:112–25.

———. 1994. "'How Do I Stop This Thing': Closure and Indeterminacy in Interactive Narratives." In *Hyper/Text/Theory*, edited by George P. Landow, 159–88. Baltimore: Johns Hopkins University Press.

Eber, Irene. 1979. Introduction to Richard Wilhelm, *Lectures on the I Ching: Constancy and Change*. Princeton: Princeton University Press.

Eco, Umberto. 1976. *A Theory of Semiotics*. Bloomington: Indiana University Press.

———. 1979. *The Role of the Reader: Explorations in the Semiotics of Texts*. Bloomington: Indiana University Press.

———. 1984. *Semiotics and the Philosophy of Language*. London: Macmillan.

———. 1989. *The Open Work.* Cambridge: Harvard University Press.

———. 1994. *Six Walks in the Fictional Woods.* Cambridge: Harvard University Press.

Elmer-De Witt, Philip, and Jamie Murphy. 1983. "Computers: Putting Fiction on a Floppy." *TIME,* December 5.

Engst, Adam. 1989. *Descent into the Maelstrom.* Shareware hyperfiction, distributed by the author.

Eriksen, Thomas Hylland. 1994. "En ny, interessant blanding!" An interview with Vikram Seth. *Samtiden,* June, 28–38.

Ernst, Josef. 1992. "Computer Poetry: An Act of Disinterested Communication." *New Literary History* 23:451–65.

Etter, Thomas, and William Chamberlain. 1984. *Racter.* Northbrook, Ill.: Mindscape.

Feenberg, Andrew. 1991. *Critical Theory of Technology.* Oxford: Oxford University Press.

Firstenberg, Allen S. 1995. *The Unending Addventure.* WWW game started February 12, 1995. Available on the Internet. http://www.addventure. com/addventure/

Fish, Stanley. 1980. "Interpreting the Variorum." In *Reader-Response Criticism: From Formalism to Post-Structuralism,* edited by Jane P. Tompkins, 164–84. Baltimore: Johns Hopkins University Press.

Foner, Leonard N. 1993. "What's an Agent, Anyway? A Sociological Case Study." Available on the Internet. http://foner.www.media.mit.edu/ people/foner/Julia/Julia.html

Fontanier, Pierre. 1968 (1821–30). *Les figures du discours.* Paris: Flammarion.

Foucault, Michel. 1973. *The Order of Things: An Archaeology of the Human Sciences.* New York: Vintage.

———. 1988. "What Is an Author?" In *Modern Criticism and Theory,* edited by David Lodge, 196–210. New York: Longman.

Gadamer, Hans-Georg. 1989 (1960). *Truth and Method.* London: Sheed and Ward.

Gay, Jonathan, and Mark Stephen Pierce. 1986. *Dark Castle.* Version 1.1. San Diego: Silicon Beach Software.

Genette, Gérard. 1980 (1972). *Narrative Discourse: An Essay in Method.* Translated by Jane E. Levin. Ithaca: Cornell University Press.

———. 1982. *Figures of Literary Discourse.* New York: Columbia University Press.

Gerrard, Peter. 1984. *Exploring Adventures on the BBC Model B.* London: Duckworth.

Gibson, William. 1986. "Burning Chrome." In *Burning Chrome.* New York: Ace Books.

———. 1992. *Agrippa: A Book of the Dead.* New York: Kevin Begos.

Graves, David. 1991. "The Automated Playwright." Paper presented at the Fifth Annual Computer Game Developer's Conference.

Greenacre, Michael J. 1984. *Theory and Applications of Correspondence Analysis*. London: Academic.

Gumbrecht, Hans Ulrich, and K. Ludwig Pfeiffer, eds. 1994. *Materialities of Communication*. Stanford: Stanford University Press.

Gundlach, Rolf. 1985. "Tempelrelief." In *Lexicon der Ägyptologie*. Vol. 6. Wiesbaden: Otto Harrassowitz.

Gygax, Gary. 1974. *Dungeons and Dragons*. Lake Geneva, N.Y.: TSR.

Hafner, Katie, and John Markoff. 1991. *Cyberpunk: Outlaws and Hackers on the Computer Frontier*. New York: Touchstone.

Hall, Trevor. 1983. *Twin Kingdom Valley*. Adventure game, published by Bug-Byte.

Haraway, Donna J. 1991 (1985). "A Cyborg Manifesto: Science, Technology, and Socialist-Feminism in the Late Twentieth Century." In *Simians, Cyborgs, and Women: The Reinvention of Nature*. New York: Routledge.

———. 1992 (1989). *Primate Visions: Gender, Race, and Nature in the World of Modern Science*. London: Verso.

Harpold, Terence. 1994. "Conclusions." In *Hyper/Text/Theory*, edited by George P. Landow, 189–222. Baltimore: Johns Hopkins University Press.

Hjelmslev, Louis. 1961. *Prologomena to a Theory of Language*. Translated by Francis J. Whitfield. Madison: University of Winsconsin Press.

Holzer, Jenny. 1993. *I Am Awake at the Place Where Women Die*. Electronic installation.

Hopkins, Sharon. 1995. "Listen." *Economist*, July 1, 1995. See also the anonymous article "Electric Metre."

Hutcheon, Linda. 1988. *A Poetics of Postmodernism: History, Theory, Fiction*. London: Routledge.

Ingarden, Roman. 1973 (1931). *The Literary Work of Art: An Investigation on the Borderlines of Ontology, Logic, and Theory of Literature*. Evanston: Northwestern University Press.

Iser, Wolfgang. 1974. *The Implied Reader: Patterns of Communication in Prose Fiction from Bunyan to Beckett*. Baltimore: Johns Hopkins University Press.

———. 1978. *The Act of Reading: A Theory of Aesthetic Response*. Baltimore: Johns Hopkins University Press.

———. 1980 (1974). "The Reading Process: A Phenomenological Approach." In *Reader-Response Criticism: From Formalism to Post-Structuralism*, edited by Jane P. Tompkins, 50–69. Baltimore: Johns Hopkins University Press.

Jakobson, Roman. 1960. "Closing Statement: Linguistics and Poetics." In *Style and Language*, edited by Thomas A. Sebeok. Cambridge: MIT Press.

Jameson, Fredric. 1991. *Postmodernism; or, the Cultural Logic of Late Capitalism.* Durham: Duke University Press.

Jenkins, Henry. 1992. *Textual Poachers: Television Fans and Participatory Culture.* New York: Routledge.

Jensen, Jens F. 1990. "Formatering af forskningsfeltet: Computer-Kultur and Computer-Semiotik." In *Computer-Kultur—Computer-Medier—Computer-Semiotik,* edited by Jens F. Jensen, 10–50. Aalborg: Nordisk Sommeruniversitet.

Johnson, B. S. 1969. *The Unfortunates.* London: Panther.

Johnson-Eilola, Johndan. 1991. " 'Trying to See the Garden': Interdisciplinary Perspectives on Hypertext Use in Composition Instruction." *Writing on the Edge,* 2:92–111.

Jones, Dave, Gary Timmons, and Scott Johnston. 1992. *Lemmings.* Liverpool: Psygnosis.

Joyce, Michael. 1988. "Siren Shapes: Exploratory and Constructive Hypertexts." *Academic Computing,* November.

———. 1990. *Afternoon: A Story.* Cambridge, Mass: Eastgate Systems.

———. 1991. "Notes Toward an Unwritten Non-Linear Electronic Text, 'The Ends of Print Culture.' " *Postmodern Culture* 2 (September): 45 numbered paragraphs.

Kac, Eduardo. 1995. *Holopoetry: Essays, Manifestoes, Critical and Theoretical Writings.* Lexington, Mass.: New Media Editions.

Kelley, Robert T. 1993. "A Maze of Twisty Little Passages, All Alike: Aesthetics and Teleology in Interactive Computer Fictional Environments." *Science-Fiction Studies* 20:52–68.

Kelso, Margaret Thomas, Peter Weyhrauch, and Joseph Bates. 1992. "Dramatic Presence." Technical Report CMU-CS-92-195, School of Computer Science, Carnegie Mellon University, Pittsburgh.

Kendall, Robert. 1996. "Hypertextual Dynamics in a Life Set for Two." In *Hypertext '96: Proceedings.* Association for Computing Machinery. Available on the Internet. http://ourworld.compuserve.com/homepages/rkendall/ht96.htm

Kermode, Frank. 1967. *The Sense of an Ending: Studies in the Theory of Fiction.* Oxford: Oxford University Press.

Landow, George P. 1991. "The Rhetoric of Hypermedia: Some Rules for Authors." In *Hypermedia and Literary Studies,* edited by Paul Delany and George P. Landow, 81–104. Cambridge: MIT Press.

———. 1992a. *Hypertext: The Convergence of Contemporary Literary Theory and Technology.* Baltimore: Johns Hopkins University Press.

———. 1992b. "Hypertext, Metatext, and the Electronic Canon." In *Literacy Online: The Promise (and Peril) of Reading and Writing with Computers,* edited by Myron C. Tuman, 67–94. Pittsburgh: University of Pittsburgh Press.

Lanestedt, Jon. 1989. *Episk Programvare—En Litterær Teksttype?* Oslo: University of Oslo.

Lanestedt, Jon, and George P. Landow. 1992. *The In Memoriam Web.* Cambridge, Mass.: Eastgate Systems.

Lanham, Richard A. 1989. "The Electronic Word: Literary Study and the Digital Revolution." *New Literary History* 20:265–90.

———. 1993. *The Electronic Word: Democracy, Technology, and the Arts.* Chicago: University of Chicago Press.

Laurel, Brenda Kay. 1986. "Toward the Design of a Computer-Based Interactive Fantasy System." Ph.D. diss., Ohio State University.

———. 1991. *Computers as Theatre.* Reading, Mass.: Addison-Wesley.

Levy, Steven. 1984. *Hackers: Heroes of the Computer Revolution.* New York: Dell.

———. 1992. *Artificial Life: The Quest for a New Creation.* New York: Pantheon.

Liddil, Bob. 1981. "Interactive Fiction: Six Micro Stories." *Byte* 6.

Liestøl, Gunnar. 1994. "Wittgenstein, Genette, and the Reader's Narrative in Hypertext." In *Hyper/Text/Theory,* edited by George P. Landow, 87–120. Baltimore: Johns Hopkins University Press.

Lodge, David. 1977. *The Modes of Modern Writing: Metaphor, Metonymy, and the Typology of Modern Literature.* London: Edward Arnold.

Lyons, Joan, ed. 1985. *Artists' Books: A Critical Anthology and Sourcebook.* Rochester, N.Y.: Visual Studies Workshop Press; Layton, Utah: Peregrine Smith.

McHale, Brian. 1987. *Postmodernist Fiction.* New York: Methuen.

———. 1992. *Constructing Postmodernism.* London: Routledge.

McKinnon, A. 1989. "Mapping the Dimensions of a Literary Corpus." *Literary and Linguistic Computing* 4:73–84.

McLuhan, Marshall. 1964. *Understanding Media: The Extensions of Man.* New York: Penguin.

Maldonado, Tomás. 1993. *Virkelig og virtuell.* Translated by Roy Eriksen. Oslo: Aschehoug kursiv.

Martin, Wallace. 1986. *Recent Theories of Narrative.* Ithaca: Cornell University Press.

Mauldin, Michael L. 1994. "Chatterbots, Tinymuds, and The Turing Test: Entering the Loebner Prize Competition." Paper presented at the American Association for Artificial Intelligence annual meeting. Available on the Internet. http://fuzine.mt.cs.cmu.edu/mlm/aaai94.html

Meehan, James Richard. 1976. "The Metanovel: Writing Stories by Computer." Ph.D. diss., Yale University.

Melville, Herman. 1851. *Moby Dick; or, The Whale.* London.

Miller, J. Hillis. 1992. *Illustration.* Cambridge: Harvard University Press.

Motte, Warren F., trans. and ed. 1986. *OuLiPo: A Primer of Potential Literature*. Lincoln: University of Nebraska Press.

Moulthrop, Stuart. 1989. "Hypertext and 'the Hyperreal.'" In *Hypertext '89: Proceedings*, 259–67. New York: Association for Computing Machinery.

————. 1991a. "Reading from the Map: Metonymy and Metaphor in the Fiction of Forking Paths." In *Hypermedia and Literary Studies*, edited by Paul Delany and George P. Landow, 119–32. Cambridge: MIT Press.

————. 1991b. "You Say You Want a Revolution? Hypertext and the Laws of Media." *Postmodern Culture* 1 (May), 53 numbered paragraphs.

————. 1991c. *Victory Garden*. Cambridge, Mass: Eastgate Systems.

————. 1991d. "Polymers, Paranoia, and the Rhetoric of Hypertext." *Writing on the Edge* 2:150–59.

————. 1994a. "Rhizome and Resistance: Hypertext and the Dreams of a New Culture." In *Hyper/Text/Theory*, edited by George P. Landow, 299–319. Baltimore: Johns Hopkins University Press.

————. 1994b. "Interactive Fiction." In *The Encyclopedia of English Studies and Language Arts*, edited by A. Purves. Jefferson City, Mo.: Scholastic.

————. 1994c. "Fearful Circuitry: Landow's Hypertext." *Computers and the Humanities* 28:53–62.

————. 1995. *Hegirascope*. Available on the World Wide Web. http://raven.ubalt.edu/Moulthrop/hypertexts/HGS/Hegirascope.html

Moulthrop, Stuart, and Nancy Kaplan. 1991. "Something to Imagine: Literature, Composition, and Interactive Fiction." *Computers and Composition* 9 (November): 7–23.

Mowitt, John. 1992. *Text: The Genealogy of an Antidisciplinary Object*. Durham: Duke University Press.

Murray, Janet H. 1991. "Anatomy of a New Medium: Literary and Pedagogic Uses of Advanced Linguistic Computer Structures." *Computers and the Humanities* 25:1–14.

————. 1995. "The Pedagogy of Cyberfiction: Teaching a Course on Reading and Writing Interactive Narrative." In *Contextual Media: Multimedia and Interpretation*, edited by Edward Barrett and Marie Redmond, 129–62. Cambridge: MIT Press.

Nabokov, Vladimir. 1962. *Pale Fire*. London: Penguin.

Nelson, Theodor Holm. 1965. "A File Structure for the Complex, the Changing, and the Indeterminate." In *Proceedings of the 20th National Conference*, 84–100. New York: Association for Computing Machinery.

————. 1987. *Literary Machines*. Edition 87.1. Available from author at P.O. Box 128, Swarthmore PA, 19091, USA.

————. 1992. "Opening Hypertext: A Memoir." In *Literacy Online: The Promise (and Peril) of Reading and Writing with Computers*, edited by Myron C. Tuman, 43–57. Pittsburgh: University of Pittsburgh Press.

Niesz, Anthony J., and Norman N. Holland. 1984. "Interactive Fiction." *Critical Inquiry* 11:110–29.

Ong, Walter J. 1982. *Orality and Literacy: The Technologizing of the Word.* London: Routledge.

OuLiPo (Ouvroir de Littérature Potentielle). 1981. *Atlas de Littérature Potentielle.* Paris: Gallimard.

Pavic, Milorad. 1990. *Landscape Painted with Tea.* New York: Knopf.

Persson, Hans. 1995. "Information about Interactive Fiction Games." Available on the Internet. ftp.gmd.de as /if-archive/info/adventure-game-history

Porush, David. 1985. *The Soft Machine: Cybernetic Fiction.* New York: Methuen.

———. 1989. "Cybernetic Fiction and Postmodern Science." *New Literary History* 20:373–96.

Poster, Mark. 1990. *The Mode of Information: Poststructuralism and Social Context.* Cambridge, Mass.: Polity Press.

Queneau, Raymond. 1961. *Cent mille milliards de poèmes.* Paris: Gallimard.

Rand, Ayn. 1936. *Night of January 16th.* New York: Longmans, Green.

Randall, Neil. 1988. "Determining Literariness in Interactive Fiction." *Computers and the Humanities* 22:182–91.

Reid, Elizabeth M. 1991. "Electropolis: Communication and Community on Internet Relay Chat." Honors thesis, University of Melbourne. Available on the Internet. http://www.ee.mu.oz.au/papers/emr/

———. 1994. "Cultural Formations in Text-Based Virtual Realities." Master's thesis, University of Melbourne. Available on the Internet. http://www.ee.mu.oz.au/papers/emr/

Renear, Allen. 1995. "Understanding (Hyper)Media: Required Readings." *Computers and the Humanities* 29:389–407.

Rheingold, Howard. 1991. *Virtual Reality.* New York: Summit.

Ritsema, Rudolf, and Stephen Karcher. 1994. *I Ching: The Classic Chinese Oracle of Change.* Shaftesbury, U.K.: Element Books.

Romero, John, John Carmack, and Adrian Carmack. 1993. *Doom.* Id Software. Available on the Internet. http://www.idsoftware.com/

Rosenberg, Martin E. 1994. "Physics and Hypertext: Liberation and Complicity in Art and Pedagogy." In *Hyper/Text/Theory,* edited by George P. Landow, 268–98. Baltimore: Johns Hopkins University Press.

Saporta, Marc. 1962. *Composition No. 1, Roman.* Paris: Seuil.

Schank, Roger C., with Peter Childers. 1984. *The Cognitive Computer. On Language, Learning, and Artificial Intelligence.* Reading, Mass.: Addison-Wesley.

Sebeok, Thomas A. 1991. *A Sign Is Just a Sign.* Bloomington: Indiana University Press.

Shannon, C., and W. Weaver. 1969. *The Mathematical Theory of Communication.* Urbana: University of Illinois Press.

Sherrill, Wallace A., and Wen Kuan Chu. 1989 (1977). *An Anthology of I Ching.* London: Arkana/Penguin.

Slatin, John. 1991. "Reading Hypertext: Order and Coherence in a New Medium." In *Hypermedia and Literary Studies,* edited by Paul Delany and George P. Landow, 153–69. Cambridge: MIT Press.

Sloane, Sarah Jane. 1991. "Interactive Fiction, Virtual Realities, and the Reading-Writing Relationship." Ph.D. diss., Ohio State University.

Smith, Mark, and Jamie Thomson. 1986. *Falcon 5: The Dying Sun.* London: Sphere.

Sørenssen, Bjørn. 1993. "Hypertext: From Modern Utopia to Postmodern Dystopia?" In *The Computer as Medium,* edited by Peter Bøgh Andersen, Berit Holmquist, and Jens F. Jensen, 477–90. Cambridge: Cambridge University Press.

Spilling, Pål. 1995. "Fra ARPANET til internett: En utvikling sett med norske øyne." Available on the Internet. http://nextstat2.hiof.no/isocno/social/arpa-no.html

Springer, Claudia. 1991. "The Pleasure of the Interface." *Screen* 33:303–23.

Stone, Allucquere Rosanne. 1991. "Will the Real Body Please Stand Up? Boundary Stories about Virtual Cultures." In *Cyberspace: First Steps,* edited by Michael Benedikt, 81–118. Cambridge: MIT Press.

Strand, Randi. 1992a. *Norisbo.* Original artwork. Wood print on semitransparent paper. Described in Randi Strand, *Form og Materialvalgs Betyding for Opplevelsen av Boka.* Bergen: School of Art and Design, 1992.

———. 1992b. *Form og Materialvalgs Betyding for Opplevelsen av Boka.* Bergen: School of Art and Design.

Toy, Michael, Glenn Wichman, and Ken Arnold. 1980. *Rogue.* Many versions for many computer systems available on the Internet.

Tuman, Myron C. 1992. *Word Perfect: Literacy in the Computer Age.* Pittsburgh: University of Pittsburgh Press.

Vuillemin, Alain 1990. *Informatique et littérature—1950-1990.* Paris: Champion-Slatkine.

Waterfield, Robin, and Wilfred Davies. 1988. *The Money Spider.* London: Penguin.

Weizenbaum, Joseph. 1966. Eliza. Computer program. Many versions for many computer systems available on the Internet.

Wiener, Norbert. 1948. *Cybernetics; or, Control and Communication in the Animal and the Machine.* New York: Technology Press.

Wilhelm, Richard. 1979. *Lectures on the I Ching: Constancy and Change.* Translated from the German by Irene Eber. Princeton: Princeton University Press.

———. 1989 (1923). *I Ching or Book of Changes.* Translated by R. W. (and from the German by Cary F. Baynes, 1950). Foreword by C. G. Jung. London: Arkan/Penguin.

Williams, Noel. 1992. "Computers and Writing." In *Computers and Written Texts,* edited by Christopher Butler, 247–66. Oxford: Blackwell.

Wilson, Robin J. 1983. *Introduction to Graph Theory.* New York: Longman.

Winner, Langdon. 1986. *The Whale and the Reactor: A Search for Limits in an Age of High Technology.* Chicago: University of Chicago Press.

Winograd, Ken. 1993. *Brickles Plus.* Manchester, N.H.: Space-Time Associates.

Ziegfeld, Richard. 1989. "Interactive Fiction: A New Literary Genre?" *New Literary History* 20:341–72.

Index

Library of Congress Cataloging-in-Publication Data

Aarseth, Espen J., 1965–

Cybertext : perspectives on ergodic literature / Espen J. Aarseth.

p.   cm.

Includes bibliographical references and index.

ISBN 0-8018-5578-0 (alk. paper). — ISBN 0-8018-5579-9 (pbk. : alk.
paper)

1. Discourse analysis, Literary—Data processing.   2. Literature and
technology.   3. Communication and technology.   I. Title.

P302.5.A18   1997

802'.85—dc21   97-3554

CIP

Learning Resources
Centre